THE IDEOLOGY AND PROGRAM OF THE PERUVIAN APRISTA MOVEMENT

THE IDEOLOGY AND PROGRAM OF THE PERUVIAN APRISTA MOVEMENT

BY

HARRY KANTOR

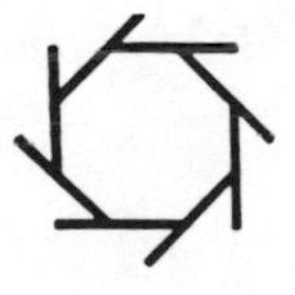

1966

OCTAGON BOOKS, INC.

New York

Originally published 1953 by University of California Press

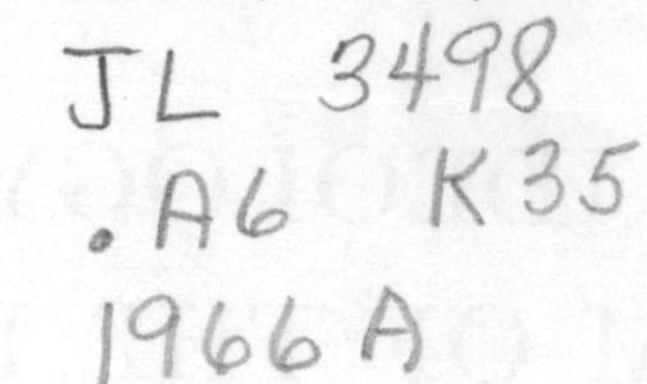

Reprinted 1966
by special arrangement with University of California Press

OCTAGON BOOKS, INC.
175 Fifth Avenue
New York, N. Y. 10010

Library of Congress Catalog Card Number: 66-18049

Printed in U.S.A. by
NOBLE OFFSET PRINTERS, INC.
NEW YORK 3, N. Y.

PREFACE

THE AUTHOR is indebted to many people for aid in the preparation of this study. Particular mention should be made of Víctor Raúl Haya de la Torre, who encouraged the writer to undertake it. During long discussions in 1948 he clarified many aspects of Aprista ideology and made it possible for the author to understand better the voluminous writings published during the past thirty years by and about the Apristas. Professor Russell H. Fitzgibbon of the University of California at Los Angeles offered generous aid and constructive advice for which the writer is grateful. Thanks are due the author's wife, Vivian Rubin Kantor, for help in typing and for her encouragement during the project. Thanks are also due to the following publishers, who have been kind enough to grant permission to quote from books and periodicals to which they hold copyrights: Friendship Press for *That Other America* by John A. Mackay, New York, 1935; The Macmillan Company for *The Encyclopedia of the Social Sciences,* New York, 1932; the editors of *The Nation* for articles by Manuel Seoane in the issue of December 15, 1945, and by Pedro Hernández Zelaya in the issue of January 1, 1949; the editors of *The Political Quarterly* for an article by Boris Mirkine-Guetzevitch in the issue of April, 1934; and the editors of *Social Research* for an article by Beate Salz in the issue of November, 1944.

HARRY KANTOR

University of Florida
Gainesville, Florida
November 26, 1952

CONTENTS

CHAPTER I

A GEOPOLITICAL REVIEW OF PERU

PERU HAD a long and interesting development before it entered the orbit of Western European history in 1531. This area is one of the few in the world where topography, climate, and natural resources combined in such a way that an energetic people could develop a civilization.[1] Although there has not been sufficient archaeological investigation of Peru, it is now known that various groups inhabiting the area advanced along the road to civilization as early as the beginning of the Christian Era.[2]

About the eleventh century, the various parts of what is now Peru were unified under the leadership of a group that has gone down in history as the Incas.[3] The Incas, a vigorous tribe that originated somewhere in the high mountains to the east of the Andean plateau, conquered most of the neighboring tribes and consolidated them into the Empire of Ttahua-ntin-suyu which gave a political, economic, cultural, and religious unity to all the area from Ecuador to northern Chile. This was no easy task; for though the early civilizations of Mesopotamia, Egypt, India, and China all began in river valleys where the coöperative use of water, in part, knit people together, the Incas, on the other hand, built their society in a territory apparently unsuited for economic prosperity and political unity because of its mountainous terrain.[4]

The great achievement of the Inca Empire was that it created a civilization suitable to the area. The government could devote its energies to production and the distribution of surplus commodities because it had no problems of foreign relations. The Inca Empire was based on agriculture. Its engineers succeeded in increasing the arable area by control of the water supply through aqueducts and irrigation and by construction of terraces on the sides of the valleys. The basic unit was not the individual but the family. Groups of families were combined into communities of various sizes, each administered by certain officials. The products of each community were divided into three parts: one to the

---

[1] Some students of early man believe that such conditions have existed only in Egypt, Mesopotamia, India, China, Yucatán, and Peru.

[2] The ruins of some of these early civilizations have been preserved. A good description of ancient Peru is found in Philip Ainsworth Means, *Ancient Civilizations of the Andes* (1931).

[3] The Western world has used the name Inca to describe the entire group. The more accurate use of the word Inca describes the ruling group in the tribe centered around the emperor, who was called the Sapa Inca.

[4] Preston E. James, *Latin America* (1950), p. 128.

priests of the sun; one to the Inca; and one for the support of the community. The Inca's share provided a surplus which was stored in warehouses and was used for distribution in any part of the empire where crops failed. Private property and money were unknown or unimportant in the Inca Empire. The ownership of all land was vested in the Inca. The family dwelling, together with its contents and the land on which it stood, was regarded as belonging to its occupants as long as they desired to use it. The conception of exploitation of natural resources for personal gain was unknown to the Incas. They were skilled in weaving cloth from alpaca wool and cotton. They were fine engineers, constructing suspension bridges, irrigation ditches, terraces, and massive walls for large buildings. They were skilled workers in metal, using gold, silver, copper, and tin.[5]

The Inca Empire supported a population much greater than that which has inhabited the same area at any time since then. No exact figures exist, but Philip Ainsworth Means estimates the population of the empire to have been approximately twice what it is today.[6] Means sums up a lifetime study of the Incas by saying:

> There can be no doubt, I think, as to the relative practical merits of the Incaic system in Peru and of the Spanish colonial system which followed upon it. No one who examines the evidence regarding the two can fail to arrive at the conclusion that the subjects of the Incas were more free from oppression and misery than were their descendents under the Hapsburgs and the Bourbons.[7]

The story of how Pizarro, the untutored swineherd from Estremadura, and a handful of companions conquered the Inca Empire with its millions of inhabitants has been told many times.[8] In the process of establishing their rule the Spaniards overwhelmed the Inca state; disrupted many of the irrigation systems; and destroyed the north and south roads that helped knit the area together. In a comparatively short time they decimated the population.

What is important to bear in mind is that the Inca Empire unified the country. It developed a style of living suited to the geography of the area. The Spanish conquest stopped the orderly development of the indigenous population. The Spaniards were afflicted with a money and religious complex entirely foreign to the native population. They turned the entire development of Peru outward. They made Lima, very near to the coast, the chief city and turned the energies of the popula-

[5] Means, *op. cit., passim.*

[6] *Ibid.*, p. 296.

[7] Philip Ainsworth Means, *The Fall of the Inca Empire* (1932), p. 288.

[8] William H. Prescott's *History of the Conquest of Peru* is one of the best accounts.

tion toward production of minerals and crops valuable in Spain. Everything in Peru was supposed to revolve around Spain.

Despite a determined effort, three hundred years of Spanish rule in Peru failed to transform the Indian population into Europeans on the Spanish model.[9] The Spanish language became predominant, but millions of Indians failed to adopt the language. Roman Catholicism was introduced, but the mass of Indians were but imperfectly Christianized. The Spanish land system encouraged and permitted concentration of large agrarian holdings in the hands of the Church and the nobility who cultivated their lands in an indifferent fashion. An aristocracy of wealth and privilege was solidly established. Communications were slow and uncertain. Little was done to educate the masses. A large number of officials and a tradition of graft laid the foundations for many future ills.[10]

The revolution against Spain in America found Peru a staunch supporter of Spain. Peru was the last country in South America to win its independence. "Here the *penates* of Spain were preserved: the treasure, the vigilant aristocracy, the warlike armies. It was not until 1824, when America was already independent, that the victory of Ayacucho liberated Peru from the Spanish rule."[11] It was not Peruvians who freed Peru; it was San Martín, who came from the south with his Argentine and Chilean troops, and Bolívar and Sucre, who came from the north with their troops.

For Peru, independence from Spain had one main effect—the composition of the ruling group was changed from Spaniards born in Spain to Spaniards born in Peru. The economic and social life of the country continued as before. Two main groups lived side by side. The Indians lived on a self-sufficient, primitive, communal, and superstitious basis; they remained closely adjusted to the land and indifferent to the politics and progress of the rest of the country. The rest of the population, especially that section in and around Lima and along the coast, lived under more modern conditions. Large and technically efficient cotton and sugar plantations and large mining enterprises owned by foreign capital gave the coast a character foreign to the "other Peru," the Peru of the indigenous population.

Beate Salz described the social stratification in this area: ". . . on one side, a white, Spanish-descended, numerically small, dominant minority

[9] Frank Tannnebaum, "Agrarismo, indianismo, y nacionalismo," *Hispanic American Historical Review*, XXIII (August, 1943), 399.

[10] J. Fred Rippy, *Historical Evolution of Hispanic America* (1932), pp. 113–114.

[11] F. García Calderón, *Latin America: Its Rise and Progress* (1913), p. 113.

(eight to fifteen per cent of the total population of Peru, Bolivia, Ecuador), and on the other a vast majority, homogeneous in itself as an ethnic, historical, agrarian and, above all, politically impotent and economically underprivileged group. The two are culturally alien to each other. Although the Catholic Church has imposed its creed upon the Indians, and has effected an amalgamation of the Indians and the Spanish in some respects, it has not effaced what is essentially Indian. For the Indian, the Spanish-Catholic culture is but a thin patina."[12] Today the two parts of the Peruvian population are living side by side, but each way of life is incompatible with the other. Some students of the subject think the two ways of life are no nearer to mutual adjustment than at any period during the last four hundred years.[13]

This basic split in the population gives rise to most of the social problems of Peru. The Spaniards created an agriculture based on export crops that would bring a cash return. As a result it has always been necessary for modern Peru to resort to importation to supplement its foodstuffs. Cattle are still scarce and not very productive. Dairy production is insufficient to satisfy normal consumption. Cotton is the most important product of the coastal region, utilizing the labor of 100,000 persons. The entire economic life of the country is influenced by the results of the cotton harvest and the prices obtained for it on the world market. The same is true of minerals; because the products of mines bring a cash return, practically the entire mineral production is exported.[14]

The Andes divide Peru into three distinct areas: the coast, the intermontane plateaus, and the jungle east of the mountains. Each of these three parts has its own problems and its own way of living. None of the governments in the past four hundred years succeeded in uniting them into a functional whole. The Incas were the only people who welded the diverse parts of Peru together into a workable whole. They used the differences in the country as a means of furthering the prosperity of the area and ruled a well-knit empire with an integrated central authority and a functioning economy. Ever since the Spanish conquistadores destroyed the Inca Empire, Peru has lain shattered. Even modern means of transportation and communication have not served the purpose of welding the country together.[15]

[12] Beate Salz, "Indianismo," *Social Research*, XI (Nov., 1944), 447–448.

[13] James, *op. cit.*, p. 185.

[14] Peruvian Commission of Inter-American Development, *Reports Presented to the Conference of Commissions of Inter-American Development* (1944), pp. 4–7.

[15] Carleton Beals, *America South* (1937), pp. 68–69; Moisés Sáenz, after making a study of Peru, wrote, "If it is true that no capital is really representative of the

The fact that Peru economically is a colonial country adds to its problems and serves further to complicate the picture. Sixty per cent of the Peruvian railroads are owned in perpetuity by the British. A German family owns Casa Grande, which produces forty-five per cent of Peru's sugar crop. Italians own a bank and an electric power, light, and trolley monopoly in Lima. United States capital is represented by the Cerro de Pasco Copper Corporation, which mines ninety-five per cent of the copper and more than half the country's large supply of silver and gold. Other important United States firms with investments in Peru are International Petroleum and W. P. Grace and Company, which has a virtual monopoly on shipping between the United States and Peru.[16]

This then is Peru, a country split by its towering mountains, its people living two different ways of life, its chief natural resources exploited by foreign capital. The result of this combination creates an exceedingly unstable political situation. The writer of an article in the New York *Times*, in 1936, computed: "The majority of the governments in the 115 years Peru has been a republic have been either revolutionary and dictatorial, or provisional. Of the eighty-seven administrations only twenty-two have been constitutional."[17]

The question may well be asked, Why does the ruling group in Peru fail to build up the country and create a modern, integrated nation-state? The answer is that any basic change in the economic and social organization of Peru would probably jeopardize the status of the ruling group, which refuses to abandon its position, preferring instability and dictatorship to the gains that might accompany any change.[18] Professor Samuel Guy Inman, in 1937, described Peru as an area that "has continued to suffer from the dominance of three forces—a reactionary church hierarchy; a small colonial-minded, intellectual aris-

---

country that it governs, this is more than ever true in the case of Lima.... Lima is the center, but not central. It was the seat of Spanish colonial power; now it is the seat of the government. Spiritually the *Sierra* is not with Lima. 'They founded it next to the sea, that it might look out toward Spain; ever since it has looked toward the outside world, courting foreigners; it is the sweetheart of the sailors of the seven seas; it is not ours. They write books about the Indians but only because it is fashionable. What does Lima really know about us?' Thus speak the men of Cuzco." *The Peruvian Indian* (1944), p. 10.

[16] Samuel Guy Inman, *Latin America, Its Place in World Life* (rev. ed., 1942), pp. 166–167.

[17] New York *Times*, Nov. 16, 1936, p. 2.

[18] Professor Blanksten found a similar situation in Ecuador. He reports that any change toward constitutional stability requires a program which would run counter to the short-range vital interests of the ruling group. Therefore, the ruling group in Ecuador prefers to retain its present dominance and political instability. George I. Blanksten, *Ecuador: Constitutions and Caudillos* (1951), *passim.*

tocracy; and a narrow, Lima-centered government group that forgets the provinces."[19]

In the history of Peru, politics was a contest among military leaders, rich landowners, and agents of foreign capital to see which group would gain the privilege of getting the graft and spoils of office. Political parties—as that term is understood in the United States—did not exist. The Aprista movement is an attempt to create a political organization that can find solutions to the problems that confront Peru.[20] A systematic review of the ideology and program advocated by the Aprista movement has never been made. This study, based upon the writings of the Aprista leaders, attempts to remedy that situation.

---

[19] Samuel Guy Inman, *Latin America, Its Place in World Life* (1937), p. 140.

[20] Little accurate information is available about the problems of Peru. When *Fortune* made a study of Peru in 1938, it reported, "To the inquiring economist Peru is just as baffling at first glimpse as it is to the sight-seeing tourist, for even after centuries of Europeanization Pizarro's land has not learned how to keep records or statistics. There has been no census of Peru since 1876. [One was finally taken in 1940.] The Government probably knows more about foreign industries than it does about its own; and vice versa, the foreigners know more about economic Peru than the Government does. Everywhere the investigator turns the most elementary figures are lacking. Consequently Peru must be studied in pieces; the mysterious whole can only be guessed." "South America II: Peru," *Fortune*, vol. 17 (Jan., 1938), 52–53.

CHAPTER II

A HISTORICAL SKETCH OF THE APRISTA MOVEMENT

THE APRISTA movement developed during the period of unrest that followed the First World War, although its intellectual origins go back to the Peru of the nineteenth century.[1] The group of young Peruvians who were to create the Aprista movement began their association with little political awareness. Without planning for political activity, they coöperated as students interested in education; the force of events developed their movement into a political party.

The time was just after the First World War, a period of great ferment in Latin America as in other parts of the world. As a result of the war, Europe had lost some of its glamour for the Latin American intellectuals, who began to realize that Europe was not the ideal many had considered it to be. The Mexican revolution, the Russian revolution, and the end of war prosperity contributed to the state of unrest. One conspicuous result of the ferment in Latin America was the beginning of a radical student movement. It started in July, 1918, with a student strike at the University of Córdoba, Argentina, for the purpose of modernizing the school. The strike of the Argentine students was accompanied by violence and received sympathy all over Latin America. It ended when the Argentine government acceded to the demands of the students, and the organization of a modern university system began in the Argentine.[2]

The Córdoba student movement seems to have been the spark which stimulated similar activity in other countries and led to the creation of organized student movements in many of the Latin American republics.[3] Víctor Raúl Haya de la Torre called this student movement "a vast intellectual renaissance,"[4] and José Carlos Mariátegui wrote that "it pointed to the birth of the new Latin American generation."[5] It marked a turning point in Latin American life, and in Peru the student movement was to lead to the creation of a new political movement—Aprismo.

[1] Robert Edwards McNicoll, "Intellectual Origins of Aprismo," *Hispanic American Historical Review*, XXIII (August, 1943), 424.

[2] Víctor Raúl Haya de la Torre, "Latin America's Student Revolution," *The Bulletin of the Pan American Union*, vol. 60 (Nov., 1926), 1105–1108.

[3] *Loc. cit.* The complete story of the student movement can be found in Gabríel del Mazo, *La reforma universitaria* (1926–1927), six volumes.

[4] Haya de la Torre, *op. cit.*, p. 1105.

[5] José Carlos Mariátegui, *7 ensayos de interpretación de la realidad peruana* (1934), p. 104.

In Peru the student movement began, at the beginning of 1919, with a struggle to reform the University of San Marcos in Lima. The students organized a strike which was supported by the workers of Lima. They demanded, among other things, a reorganization of the university, the dismissal of sixteen professors, academic freedom, and the participation of the students in the governing councils of the university. The students' strike lasted four months, ending when the Peruvian legislature voted reform laws for the university.[6]

The student-worker alliance and the organizations created during the strike were to become the basis of the Peruvian Aprista movement. Víctor Raúl Haya de la Torre, who was to become the *jefe* of the Aprista movement, was twenty-four and a half years old when he was elected president of the San Marcos Federation of Students.[7] Manuel Seoane, another leader of the Apristas, who was to be the first vice-president of the Senate many years later, was then also a student, as were many others who were to become active political leaders when the Aprista movement was organized.

A congress of Peruvian students met in Cuzco in March, 1920. Students from the schools in Lima, Arequipa, and Cuzco met together for the first time to discuss their mutual problems.[8] At this congress the idea of having the college students create an adult education movement was broached. The students adopted the idea and founded night schools for workers called the Universidades Populares González Prada. Here the workers studied social problems and learned to defend the rights of the Indians. Each college student was asked to give some time to teaching in these adult centers. The popular universities were a success.[9] The contact between the students and the workers in these schools served to solidify the alliance created during the students' strike.

The student movement was the direct predecessor of the Aprista movement, but the intellectual origins of the movement, as already mentioned, reach back into the events and ideas of the nineteenth century. Three men, in particular, have been sources of inspiration for the Apristas: Francisco de Paula González Vigil (1792–1875); Manuel González Prada (1846–1918); and José Carlos Mariátegui (1895–1930).[10]

González Vigil was a scholar and statesman who struggled for a better

[6] Haya de la Torre, *op. cit.*, pp. 1106–1107.

[7] Luis Alberto Sánchez, *Raúl Haya de la Torre o el político* (1934), p. 64.

[8] *Ibid.*, pp. 66–67.

[9] A brief history of these schools, written by an Aprista, is found in *Almanaque la tribuna 1948*, pp. 183–184.

[10] Partido Aprista Peruano, *El proceso Haya de la Torre* (1933), pp. xxxviii–xl.

Peru in the first years of her independence. He opposed the *caudillos* and was Peru's most famous atheist, famous for his attacks upon the evil effects of religious ignorance on free thought. For his efforts he suffered imprisonment and exile, and he was excommunicated by the Roman Catholic Church for writing his *Defensa de la autoridad de los gobiernos contra las pretensiones de la Curia Romana* (12 vols., 1848-1856). His was a lone voice crying in the wilderness, but the Apristas look upon him as "the first of the precursors of the new Peru."[11]

Peru's defeat by Chile in the War of 1879–1883 acted as a stimulus to awaken the intellectual leaders of the country, since losing the war was a great shock to them. Peru's colonial-minded rulers looked upon themselves as the inheritors of the glory of the Viceroyalty of Peru. During the war the Chileans defeated their armies, captured Lima, the City of Kings, and took away a part of Peru's territory.

When the war was over some of the more alert thinkers began to discuss among themselves the reasons for the defeat of Peru. These discussions, stimulated by the military defeat, brought into being critics of Peruvian society who produced what Jorge Basadre called "literature of disillusionment."[12] Four main themes were emphasized in the writings of this group: a concern for the Indian population; a criticism of the European outlook of the creole ruling group in Lima; a criticism of the system of land tenure which made it difficult for the middle class to own land; and a criticism of the Church.[13]

The outstanding critic of the old order was Manuel González Prada. His speeches and writings stimulated a large group of younger Peruvians to dedicate themselves to the solution of the problems of Peru.[14] González Prada attacked the Church for its orthodox dogma, its clericalism, and its control of education. He raised the question of the status of the Indian; he fought for free thought; and in his later years he moved closer to the working class and declared that they would solve the social question by revolution.[15]

González Prada had a direct influence upon Haya de la Torre and some of the other students he talked to in his last years, when he was

[11] *Ibid.*, p. xxxix.

[12] Jorge Basadre, *Perú: Problema y posibilidad* (1931), p. 156.

[13] McNicoll, *op. cit.*, pp. 424–425.

[14] González Prada's writings include: *Anarquía* (1936); *Bajo el oprobio* (1933); *Figuras y figurones* (1938); *Horas de lucha* (2d ed., 1924); *Nuevas páginas libres* (1937); *Páginas libres* (new ed., 1946); *Pensamientos* (1941); *Propaganda y ataque* (1939). One of the Aprista leaders, Luis Alberto Sánchez, has written a novelized biography of González Prada entitled *Don Manuel* (1937). See also William Rex Crawford, *A Century of Latin American Thought* (1944), pp. 173–182.

[15] Crawford, *op. cit.*, pp. 176–178.

the librarian of San Marcos University.[16] Alfredo Saco, an Aprista leader, refers to Manuel González Prada as the unequivocal precursor of Aprismo, especially in the political phases of his life. "Even when González Prada died in 1918," Saco writes, "before the founding of the Aprista Party, his criticisms of the political and social conditions reigning in Peru had become an inescapable antecedent of the Aprista movement which from the first made a banner of the name of 'Don Manuel.' "[17]

Inspired by González Prada and stimulated by the Argentine student movement, the student movement in Peru reached its climax in May, 1923, when the President of Peru, Augusto B. Leguía, proposed a curious ceremony, an attempt to dedicate Peru to the "Sacred Heart of Jesus." President Leguía evidently thought this act would increase his popularity and so prolong his stay in office. The students, led by Haya de la Torre, attacked this ceremony as a political maneuver. On May 23, 1923, a demonstration was organized against the government by the San Marcos students and the workers of Lima. The government attacked the demonstration; the university buildings became a battle scene as the demonstrators resisted. In the fighting, one student and one worker were killed. The union of the Lima students and workers was thus sealed in blood. The next day the Archbishop of Peru suspended the act of dedication to the "Sacred Heart of Jesus." The government closed the university; many of the student leaders were jailed or exiled from the country. Haya de la Torre was imprisoned in the prison of San Lorenzo. When he began a hunger strike to protest his illegal arrest, he was deported from the country October 9, 1923.[18]

These events were the turning point at which the student leaders began to think in terms of political action. Until the time of their deportation they thought that education could renovate the country, but their efforts had always been blocked by the government. In exile the student leaders thought about their experiences and decided to turn to political action.[19]

In Mexico City, on May 7, 1924, Haya de la Torre proposed the creation of a Popular Revolutionary Alliance for America. All Latin Americans were invited to join the new organization. It is from the initials of this name, Alianza Popular Revolucionaria Americana, that new words were coined: Apra, a short name for the organization;

[16] Sánchez, *Raúl Haya de la Torre o el político*, p. 53.
[17] In Introduction to "Aprista Bibliography: Books and Pamphlets," by Luis Alberto Sánchez and Alfredo M. Saco, *Hispanic American Historical Review*, XXIII (August, 1943), 556.
[18] Felipe Cossio del Pomar, *Haya de la Torre, el indoamericano* (1946), pp. 88–100.
[19] Alfredo Saco, *Síntesis Aprista* (1934), pp. 22–24.

Aprismo, the doctrine of the organization; Aprista, a member or follower of the organization.[20] The program of the new organization had five planks:

1. Action against Yankee imperialism.
2. For the political unity of Latin America.
3. For the nationalization of land and industry.
4. For the internationalization of the Panama Canal.
5. For solidarity with all peoples and all oppressed classes.[21]

Within this general framework each national group was to work out its own program.

The Alianza Popular Revolucionaria Americana was meant to be an organization for all Latin America. To build it, Haya de la Torre and the other founders began to spread their ideas by writing for periodicals all over the Americas. They traveled in Europe, the United States, and Latin America, talking to the numerous political exiles. One of the leaders of the new movement stated in 1929 that branches of the organization existed in Paris, London, Buenos Aires, Chile, Peru, Cuba, Puerto Rico, and San Domingo.[22]

Despite its international character, the Aprista movement made its greatest progress in Peru. This was natural since its leaders were Peruvian and conditions were ripe for its growth within their country. The movement was organized there by José Carlos Mariátegui, who is looked upon, by the Apristas, as the third of the great stimulators of free thought in Peru.

Mariátegui was a poverty-stricken tubercular who grew up in the slums of Lima. His formal schooling ended at twelve when he entered a Lima print shop as a copy boy. His further education was obtained informally through reading, yet by the time he was eighteen he was working as a journalist. As a reward for supporting President Leguía in the election of 1918, Mariátegui received a government fellowship for study and travel in Europe. A stay in postwar Europe introduced

[20] Sánchez, *Raúl Haya de la Torre o el político*, pp. 108–109.
[21] *Ibid.*, p. 109.
[22] New York *Times*, Aug. 20, 1929, p. 3. There are in existence at the present time a group of organizations that can be called Aprista, but none of them use the name in their official titles. Included among these organizations are the Acción Democrática, Venezuela; the Partido Feberista, Paraguay; the Partido Revolucionario Cubano (Auténtico), Cuba; the Partido Acción Revolucionario, Guatemala. All of these organizations advocate policies that are generally similar. They have sometimes coöperated, particularly in the creation of a League of Democratic and Socialist Parties, to which they, the Peruvian Apristas, and the Chilean Socialist party belong. See Robert J. Alexander, "Aprismo—Is it Socialist?," *Modern Review*, vol. 1 (Nov., 1947), 682–690.

him to the socialist ideology, and he returned to Peru a confirmed Marxist.[23]

Mariátegui participated in the student movement of the 1920's, which threw him into contact with the student leaders. When they were exiled from Peru, Mariátegui became the leading spokesman for the disinherited within Peru. His writings in the periodical *Amauta* and his book *7 ensayos de interpretación de la realidad peruana* (1928) helped to lay the basis for the idea that Peru needed her own type of socialism, based on the Indian institutions preserved within Peru. Mariátegui split with the Apristas in 1928 and founded the Partido Socialista Peruana which affiliated itself with the third international. Two years later he died at the age of thirty-five.[24]

The Aprista movement grew slowly in Peru, but the dictatorship of Leguía did not permit any way of measuring its strength. Then the world depression, which followed the Wall Street stock market crash, led to the overthrow of a series of Latin American governments in 1930 and 1931.[25] In Peru a military clique headed by Luis Sánchez Cerro took control of the government and imprisoned President Leguía.

The Partido Aprista Peruano, which was purely Peruvian, was then organized. Luis Eduardo Enríquez, who had been released from San Lorenzo prison, became general secretary. Manuel Seoane and Carlos Manuel Cox, who had been leaders of the student movement, returned from exile and became active in the organization. The Partido Aprista Peruano was not organically related to the parent Apra organization,

[23] On Mariátegui see: Waldo Frank, "A Great American," *The Nation*, vol. 130 (June 18, 1930), 704; Waldo Frank, "Two Peruvians: Dictator and Poet," *New Republic*, vol. 67 (August 12, 1931), 331–334; Samuel Guy Inman, "José Carlos Mariátegui," *Collier's Encyclopedia*, vol. 13 (1950), 144; Harold E. Davis, *Makers of Democracy in Latin America* (1945), pp. 93–95; Armando Bazán, *José Carlos Mariátegui* (1939); Maria Wiesse, *José Carlos Mariátegui* (1945).

[24] After Mariátegui died the Apristas and the Communists both claimed him as their member and tried to use his prestige to build their organizations. Despite the claims made by the polemicists of the two movements, no one, of course, knows whom Mariátegui would have supported if he had lived. This much is known: when he died, Luis Alberto Sánchez, an Aprista, was the secretary of the committee that collected money for his family. See the letter by Waldo Frank in *The Nation*, vol. 130 (June 18, 1930), 704. Furthermore, Mariátegui favorably quotes Haya de la Torre in his book, *7 ensayos de interpretación de la realidad peruana*, pp. 69, 202. In a footnote on p. 69 of this work, Mariátegui says: "After having finished this book, I found in Haya de la Torre's book, *Por la emancipación de la América Latina*, ideas that are in agreement with my own on the agrarian question in general and on the Indian community in particular. We start from the same point of view so that necessarily our conclusions must be the same." On the basis of this and the ideas presented in Mariátegui's writings, one can say that his ideas were such that he would probably have supported the Apristas had he lived.

[25] These included the Governments of Hernando Siles in Bolivia, Hipólito Irigoyen in Argentina, Washington Luis Pereira de Souza in Brazil, Harmodio Arosemena in Panama, Isidro Ayora in Ecuador, and General Carlos Ibáñez in Chile.

but its leadership, program, and tactics came from Peruvian members of the Apra organization. The Partido Aprista Peruano grew quickly as the exiles flocked home.[26]

An election was scheduled for the first Sunday in September of 1931. Two main candidates contested for the presidency, Sánchez Cerro, the leader of the army group which had deposed Leguía, and Haya de la Torre, the nominee of the Aprista party. Haya returned from Germany and toured the country explaining the Aprista program. More democracy prevailed in Peru during the electoral campaign than had been customary for many years. The Aprista party grew by leaps and bounds. Its propaganda was so successful that the ruling clique found it necessary to postpone the elections from the September date to October 11; it was then held to the accompaniment of wide-scale fraud and irregularities.

When the election was over, the Apristas felt sure they had won. The official results, however, gave Sánchez Cerro 155,378 votes, and Haya de la Torre 106,551 votes.[27] Two other candidates received small votes. Most students of Peruvian politics think that Haya was elected President in 1931.[28] Although the Apristas felt they had won the election, the party leaders decided to permit Sánchez Cerro to take office without opposing this action. The Aprista party had elected 27 members to the Congress and thought that under constitutional government it could use the next period to build its organization so that it would be sure to win the next election.

Events soon revealed that Sánchez Cerro was not interested in constitutional government. The headquarters of the Aprista party were closed by the government December 23, 1931.[29] The Aprista party deputies in the Congress of Peru were deported from the country February 20, 1932.[30] Other deportations followed.[31] The government ordered the arrest of Haya de la Torre and the executive committee of the Aprista party March 5, 1932. The next day a young student, who had been an Aprista, shot and wounded the President, Sánchez Cerro. Haya de la Torre was arrested in a suburb of Lima May 6, 1932.[32] A

[26] Sánchez, *Raúl Haya de la Torre o el político*, p. 175.

[27] "Our very exact calculations permit us to affirm that fifty thousand votes of our members were arbitrarily declared void." Víctor Raúl Haya de la Torre, *¿A dónde va Indoamérica?* (1935), p. 268.

[28] See, for example, Carleton Beals, *America South* (1937), p. 400; Hugo Fernández Artucio, *The Nazi Underground in South America* (1942), p. 220; Hubert Herring, *Good Neighbors* (1941), p. 267.

[29] New York *Times*, Dec. 24, 1931, p. 4.

[30] *Ibid.*, Feb. 21, 1932, p. 2.

[31] *Ibid.*, Feb. 25, 1932, p. 5.

[32] Partido Aprista Peruano, *op. cit.*, p. 29.

revolt in the city of Trujillo in July, 1932, was defeated by the combined strength of the army, navy, and air force.[33] As an aftermath of the revolt, many Apristas were assassinated. With most of its leaders in jail or in exile and with all democratic rights abrogated, the Aprista movement became quiet.

Sánchez Cerro was assassinated April 30, 1933, by an individual who, some writers claim, was a member of the Aprista party.[34] Another militarist, Oscar Benavides, seized the presidency. The Aprista movement remained outlawed until August 9, 1933, when two laws were passed by the Peruvian government. One was an amnesty law freeing political prisoners; the other was a law barring persons affiliated with international organizations from running for office. The latter measure was a new attempt to suppress the Aprista movement by preventing its members from running for public office. The vitality of the Aprista movement was demonstrated, however, when 50,000 people greeted Haya de la Torre upon his release from jail.[35]

The Apristas immediately started to build up their organization. As Samuel Guy Inman described the activity, "Apra became a compact organization, with its press and its social, educational, and research departments. It circulated by the hundreds of thousands a carefully prepared series of pamphlets. It sent its speakers to every part of the republic. It conducted various co-operative enterprises. In Lima it operated restaurants which demonstrated how economy and cleanliness could be combined for the benefit of the public."[36]

The new-found liberty for the Aprista movement did not last long. After a few months, the new government began to use repressive measures against it which came to a head in July, 1934, when the government put a ban on demonstrations.[37] A congressional election was called for September 30, but when the date neared, the election was postponed to November 11.[38] Soon the government discovered disorder in Peru; the election was again postponed; all civil liberty was abolished; and the Aprista movement was driven underground.[39]

The Apristas managed to keep their party alive although they had to function in strict illegality. Many leaders of the party were exiled or imprisoned, but Haya de la Torre remained in hiding in Lima. On

[33] Beals, *op. cit.*, p. 401.

[34] A. Curtis Wilgus, *The Development of Hispanic America* (1941), p. 458.

[35] Samuel Guy Inman, *Latin America, Its Place in World Life* (rev. ed., 1942), p. 161.

[36] *Loc. cit.*

[37] New York *Times*, July 6, 1934, p. 5.

[38] *Ibid.*, Sept. 2, 1934, p. 8; Oct. 7, 1934, p. 8.

[39] *Ibid.*, Dec. 1, 1934, p. 1.

October 11, 1936, the government felt sure enough of itself to arrange a presidential election. The Aprista movement was declared illegal and not permitted to run a candidate. The Apristas supported, therefore, one of the four candidates permitted on the ballot; the candidate supported by them was elected. The government thereupon declared the election invalid and extended the term in office of President Benavides.[40]

The Aprista movement continued to function in the underground after 1936. In 1939, the government organized an uncontested election and installed its choice for President, Manuel Prado y Ugarteche. The Apristas apparently did not participate in this election. Their leaders were either in hiding, in jail, or in exile.[41] Activities during this period, which lasted until the summer of 1945, have been described as consisting mainly in distributing leaflets and clandestine newspapers, and in mouth-to-mouth messages.[42]

In this way the years passed with the dictatorial government using force to stifle the aspirations of the people.[43] As a result of the Second World War, a modicum of prosperity came to Peru, and the political situation quieted down. That is not to say that democracy came to Peru, but rather that relations between the government and the people relaxed a little. Revolts were still blamed on the Aprista party, but the revolts were petty affairs.[44]

A new period in Peruvian politics began with the organization of a

[40] Luis Antonio Eguiguren, the man elected President who was not permitted to take office, tells his story of the election in *El usurpador* (1939).

[41] *Political Prisoners under the Dictatorship in Peru,* a pamphlet published in 1940 by the International Committee for Political Prisoners, criticizes the Peruvian government and gives a list of newspapers suppressed by the government, the names of political prisoners, and other similar information.

[42] New York *Times,* August 15, 1943, p. 38.

[43] A confidential report issued by the office of the Coördinator for Inter-American Affairs, on August 28, 1944, reads: "The Prado administration has never been strong since its inauguration in 1939, at which time observers doubted that it would last a year. It is a regime based on class control, with its main support from the so-called 'Civilista' group who dominate commerce, large-scale agriculture, industry and finance in Peru. . . . The Civilistas have maintained control since 1930 only by outlawing the powerful Alianza Popular Revolucionaria Americana (commonly called Apra) and the small but well-organized Communist Party. By fostering disunity in the opposition (for example, encouraging the Communists in 1942 to make a press attack upon the middle-class Apristas in return for certain concessions) and by employing a very strict censorship of press and radio, the Prado administration, with the aid of the army and police, has managed to retain a precarious hold on the Government." United States. Coördinator of Inter-American Affairs, *Present Political Situation in Peru, Summary.* Confidential Political Report number CR-103 (August 28, 1944), p. 3.

[44] As, for example, when on March 19, 1945, a communique of the Ministry of Government and Police announced that an attempted uprising at the Navy Air Base of Ancón was prevented by the Minister of Aeronautics, who talked the rebels out of revolting. Reported in *Andean Air Mail and Peruvian Times,* March 23, 1945, p. 2. Hereafter cited as *Peruvian Times.*

"National Democratic Front" during 1944.[45] Led by a sixty-nine-year-old poet, Dr. José Gálvez, the Democratic Front was an attempt to unite the Aprista movement and all those in Peru who, though not Apristas, desired constitutional government.[46] The Democratic Front nominated Dr. José Luis Bustamante y Rivero, a college professor who was serving as ambassador to Bolivia, for President in March, 1945. The unity of the opposition had an effect, since the government lifted the ban on the Aprista movement in May.[47] The Apristas celebrated their legalization with a demonstration on May 20, which, according to a contemporary report, consisted of between 150,000 and 200,000 people (about one-fifth of Lima's population).[48] Haya de la Torre presented the viewpoint of the Apristas upon being legalized. He said:

> We return to legal status without rancor or reproaches. Because the sufferings of 15 years of struggle for an ideal, which was destined to triumph in the world, affords sufficient compensation in the historic fact of this victory.... Peru requires a vigorous democratic structure, and the Party of the People is the basis of this. The renaissance of the country cannot be undertaken with transitory minor parties of the eleventh hour, hastily constituted each time that elections approach. Democracy assumes true parties; parties based on principles and organized with discipline and education.... Without liberty there is no social justice and we aspire to create an authentic social justice—our own—not one that comes from Moscow. We conceive of social justice not at the service of a foreign power, but at the service of the necessities and interests of our people....[49]

The elections took place June 30, 1945, and Dr. Bustamante y Rivero, the candidate of the Democratic Front, received 305,590 votes to 150,720 votes for General Eloy G. Ureta, the candidate supported by the incumbent oligarchy.[50] The Democratic Front also elected a majority to the two houses of the Peruvian Congress. In the Senate 35 of the 46 members elected had the support of the Democratic Front; 18 were Apristas. In the Chamber of Deputies 73 of the 101 members elected had the support of the Democratic Front; 48 were Apristas.[51]

The uninitiated observer would suppose that now Peru would live under constitutional government, for it had a democratically elected

[45] The date is given as June 5, 1944, in United States. Coördinator of Inter-American Affairs, *Current Political Developments in Peru.* Confidential Report number CR-105 (Oct. 9, 1944), p. 1. The program of the National Democratic Front and a review of the 1945 election are found in Toto Giurato, *Perú milenario*, vol. 3 (1947), pp. 898–912.

[46] "Peru's Coming Election," *Inter-American*, IV (Jan., 1945), 10–11.

[47] *Peruvian Times*, May 18, 1945, p. 1.

[48] "Five-to-one-Favorite?," *Inter-American*, IV (July, 1945), 5–6; *Peruvian Times*, May 25, 1945, p. 1.

[49] *Peruvian Times*, June 1, 1945, p. 1.

[50] *Ibid.*, July 20, 1945, front cover.

[51] *Ibid.*, Aug. 3, 1945, p. 1, supplement.

President installed in office and a congressional majority elected on the same ticket as the President. Events were to prove that this hope was illusory; three and a half years later, Dr. Bustamante would be in exile, Congress would be disbanded, and military dictatorship would again dominate Peru.

Peru in 1945 had a constitution which combined in an unusual form features taken from the presidential and parliamentary forms of government.[52] The President was elected by the voters and he appointed his cabinet, yet the Congress by the authority of Articles 172 and 173 of the Constitution could force the resignation of a minister. Article 166 required that "The Acts of government and administration of the President of the Republic are countersigned by the Minister of the respective department. Without this requisite they are null."[53] In actual practice this would mean a parliamentary form of government since the Congress could continue to censure ministers until those were appointed who had its confidence.

Professor Mirkine-Guetzevitch had foreseen this problem in 1934 when, in writing about the new Peruvian Constitution, he said:

> If these articles do not remain a dead letter, if they are honestly applied, it can be held that the presidential system has suffered a defeat in Peru. The possibility of defeating the ministry and compelling it to resign puts an end to presidential autocracy. The president—if let me say again, the constitution is sincerely applied—will have the character of a parliamentary head of the state. Such a provision will have the effect of renovating the political life of Latin America. But it is clear that all depends on how the article is applied, and that is why we shall have to wait for some time before we can definitely state whether or not this combination of the presidential and parliamentary systems will effectively change the political methods and habits of Latin America.[54]

The Apristas had been planning the future of Peru for many years, and now that they had an opportunity to influence the course of events they wanted to go to work. If the President and the Army had cooperated, political life would have developed normally. But they did not; in fact a minority of Congress would not even attend sessions and this led to a crisis which culminated in dictatorship. The crisis arose because the Apristas, who held a majority in the Congress, wanted to enact their program into legislation. At the same time, the President felt that he was entitled to act as a strong president, forgetting that he had been elected by the votes of the Apristas. To complicate events

[52] The Peruvian Constitution is translated in Russell H. Fitzgibbon, *et al.* (eds.), *The Constitutions of the Americas* (1948), pp. 668–694.

[53] *Ibid.*, p. 685.

[54] Boris Mirkine-Guetzevitch, "Presidential System in Peru," *Political Quarterly*, vol. 5 (April, 1934), 271.

further the conservative minority, defeated in the elections, and the Communists began a full-scale attack upon the Apristas. They accused the Apristas of trying to set up a one-party state by using their majority in the Congress to pass whatever bills they favored. The result of this was crisis after crisis in the Cabinet. Three Apristas were taken into the cabinet from January 23, 1946, to January 12, 1947, but this did not help matters because they were put in charge of minor departments.

Manuel Seoane, an Aprista leader, wrote an article which clearly portrayed the dilemma facing the government and people of Peru. He said that "reaction is still strong and thirsting for revenge. And unfortunately, it owes some of its present strength to the liberals. When fascists take power, they ruthlessly wipe out their opposition; when liberals win, they invariably guarantee freedom to everyone, including their enemies of yesterday.... The Apristas ... invited the right-wing opposition to cooperate in the reconstruction program.... They declared themselves ready to cooperate with the government—and so far have used the liberties accorded them to sabotage the national unity and prepare for a new assault against the incumbent regime."[55]

The political situation came to a head when a new session of the Congress was scheduled to convene July 28, 1947, as required by the Constitution. When the Senate was called to order, a quorum was not present because the conservative members refused to attend the session.[56] This Congress would never meet again; the boycott by the conservative members was to continue until dictatorship superseded constitutional government. The Apristas' first move to break the deadlock was the organization of a general strike which was called by the Unión Sindical de Trabajadores of Lima and Callao on August 28, 1947. The strike seriously interfered with industry and commerce in both Lima and Callao. It was broken when the President proclaimed a state of siege

[55] "Conflict in Latin America," *The Nation*, vol. 161 (Dec. 15, 1945), 655. Dr. Rafael Belaúnde, President of the Cabinet and Minister of Government and Police from July 28, 1945 to January 23, 1946, came to the same conclusion. He charges that the defeated minority in the election was determined to regain its power. Therefore, he writes, they unleashed a large-scale campaign in the press against the Aprista movement. At the same time, Dr. Belaúnde continues, President Bustamante proceeded as if his personal efforts had won the presidency for him when, in fact, his election was due to the support given to his candidacy by the Aprista movement. Dr. Belaúnde charges that the failure of President Bustamante to coöperate with the party that had put him into office forced him into coöperation with the selfish minority which was endangering constitutional government in its campaign to keep its privileges. The result was dictatorship, for which Dr. Belaúnde blames the right-wing minority and President Bustamante. Rafael Belaúnde, *Apostasía democrática del gobierno peruano*, printed leaflet, dated Jan. 1, 1948. Reprinted from *Bohemia de la Habana*, Jan. 11, 1948, and *Análisis del último mensaje presidencial*, printed leaflet, dated March 19, 1948.

[56] *Peruvian Times*, Aug. 1, 1947, cover page.

which suspended the civil liberties guaranteed by Articles 56, 61, 67, and 68 of the Constitution. Numerous arrests were made and various labor centers were closed down.[57] An attempt was then made to settle the congressional impasse by direct negotiations, but nothing was achieved.[58] President Bustamante tried to negotiate the impasse, but he, too, failed.[59] The Senators continued to boycott the session; they were in a minority and knew that once fifty-five per cent attendance had been achieved to organize the Senate they would be outvoted on important legislation.

On February 28, 1948, President Bustamante appointed a new cabinet which consisted entirely of military men. The next day, he made a radio broadcast explaining his version of the crisis in the country. The basic difficulty, the President said, was that the Aprista movement wanted to institute a one-party dictatorship. He said that the mediums of propaganda of the Aprista movement "adulterate the truth, magnify certain national problems, arousing low passions of unreflective discontent and hatred, inciting openly to subversion and murderous conflict, undermining the principle of authority and creating a state of confusion and anarchy incompatible with the solidity of our institutions."[60] The President issued a decree on March 8, abolishing the existing municipal councils throughout the Republic of Peru because many Apristas were members.[61]

The government, by decree on May 25, again postponed the congressional by-elections scheduled for June 20, 1948.[62] In June, the cabinet began to press for the outlawing of the Aprista party. President Bustamante refused to agree to this, and on June 17 the all-military cabinet

[57] *Ibid.*, Aug. 29–Sept. 5, 1947, p. 1, supplement.
[58] *Ibid.*, Nov. 21, 1947, p. 1, supplement.
[59] *Ibid.*, Jan. 2, 1948, pp. 5–7.
[60] *An English Translation of the Message of the President of the Republic, Dr. José Luis Bustamante y Rivero, addressed to the Peruvian Nation on February 29, 1948*, p. 3. The identification of the Apristas with "subversion and murderous conflict" is a constant theme in the writings of the governmental officials. The author has three pamphlets about the Aprista movement issued by the Ministerio de Gobierno y Policía, Dirección de Publicidad, all printed without dates. *La verdad sobre el Apra, aprismo es comunismo* is an attempt to demonstrate that the Aprista movement is Communist by quoting excerpts from Aprista writings. Pictures of Haya de la Torre taken in Russia are used as proof of the Communist character of Aprismo. *Los crímenes del Apra* purports to be a history of all those assassinated by the Apristas. *Terrorismo Apra* was evidently published after the Odría regime took power and it, too, attempts by pictures and text to paint Aprismo as a terroristic organization. It is difficult to say what value should be given to these three pamphlets. Since dictatorial governments never have any difficulty in proving their opponents murderers, the author is inclined to withhold judgment on this until such time as both sides of the case can be heard in a court room in a democratic Peru.
[61] *Peruvian Times*, March 5, 1948, p. 1.
[62] *Ibid.*, May 28, 1948, cover page.

resigned.[63] Some of the right-wing officers who wanted to outlaw the Aprista party attempted an abortive revolution in July.[64] Constitutional guarantees were again suspended July 5, 1948. Riots took place in various parts of the country.

A revolt broke out in Callao and in the Peruvian navy on October 3, 1948. Bitter fighting took place, including aerial bombardment of the naval vessels captured by the rebels. The army overcame the revolt. President Bustamante immediately suspended all civil rights and accused the Aprista party of leading the revolt. Troops occupied the Aprista party headquarters, seized its newspaper plant, and arrested many of the Aprista leaders. The next day President Bustamante by decree outlawed the Aprista party. Within a week, more than 1,000 Apristas were in jail.[65]

Three weeks later the army deposed President Bustamante, exiled him from Peru, and instituted a military dictatorship under General Manuel A. Odría, who had been one of Bustamante's ministers.[66] This military dictatorship is still in power (early 1952) and has been recognized by the other governments of the world. Bustamante is in exile, still calling himself President of Peru.[67] Haya de la Torre is a refugee in the Colombian Embassy in Lima while the governments of Colombia and Peru argue about his status.

One of the Aprista leaders, writing under a pseudonym, accurately described the debacle in Peru, saying:

> The whole series of events in Peru, [the congressional boycott, Bustamante trying to rule by decree, the naval revolt, the Odría dictatorship] had but one cause—the resistance of Peruvian rightists, and of President Bustamante himself, to the fundamental principle that the will of the majority should prevail. In order to keep the Apristas out of the government some curious arguments had been invented. The party was accused of being "totalitarian" because it demanded "total" power by virtue of being a majority in the nation. By the same token the British Labor Party and the Democratic Party in the United States could be called totalitarian, since they exercise "total" power after winning democratic elections.
>
> The real purpose of the right was to block the Apristas' program of social reform. Peru had hardly a quarter-hectare of arable land per person, and any plan to increase

[63] *Ibid.*, June 18, 1948, p. 1 and cover page; July 2–9, 1948, p. 3.

[64] *Ibid.*, July 2–9, 1948, p. 1.

[65] *Peruvian Times*, Oct. 1–8, 1948, pp. 1–2, supplement; New York *Times*, Oct. 4, 1948, pp. 1, 6; Oct. 5, 1948, p. 9; Oct. 6, 1948, p. 11; Oct. 7, 1948, p. 5; Oct. 8, 1948, p. 19.

[66] New York *Times*, Oct. 28, 1948, pp. 1, 4; Oct. 29, 1948, p. 18; Oct. 30, 1948, pp. 1, 5; Oct. 31, 1948, p. 38.

[67] José Luis Bustamante y Rivero, *Tres años de lucha por la democracia en el Perú* (1949). In this book Dr. Bustamante tries to justify his actions during his presidency. He blames the Apristas for what happened and calls them totalitarians who wanted a single-party state.

the amount by irrigation would lessen the value of the land now available. Some 60 per cent of the people are illiterate, and if new schools taught the peasants to read and do sums, they could not be deceived so easily.

Development of the Sechura oil fields would be fatal to the cotton and sugar barons who pay wages of three and a half soles a day, for the North American oil companies pay their workers eighteen soles. These are examples of the changes Apra proposed and the right resists.

For more than a hundred years a small but powerful group has ruled the country as a vast feudal domain, and it does not want to lose its privileges. Since there are few artisans in Peru, new industries would draw the peons away from the plantations and transform docile domestic servants into restless factory workers. Democracy would bring these and other calamities to the old colonial overlords.[68]

That seems to sum up the political situation in Peru. The Apristas appear to have won the elections in 1931; they did win in 1936 by the dictatorship's own admission; they won in 1945. But each time they failed to obtain power. There are those who think that the Apristas are poor politicians; it is also possible that they have been faced by a long-established, implacable, ruthless foe which looks back to four hundred years of class domination and cannot comprehend an order in which it does not rule.

As Hernández Zelaya points out: "One cannot say what the future holds, but dark days must be expected for Peru; a country cannot always remain the property of a feudal minority which blocks all progress."[69]

[68] Pedro Hernández Zelaya, "Peru Moves Backward," *The Nation*, vol. 168 (Jan. 1, 1949), 10.

[69] *Ibid.*, p. 11.

CHAPTER III

THE DEVELOPMENT OF A PROGRAM APPLICABLE TO LATIN AMERICA

LATIN AMERICA IS NOT EUROPE

THE APRISTA ideas and program have been expounded for more than twenty-five years in hundreds of books, pamphlets, and periodicals.[1] There does not seem to be any one place, however, where the Aprista ideology has been synthesized and made available to those interested in finding out what it is. Most of the voluminous bibliography compiled by the Apristas deals with specialized aspects of their program and ideas or is of a polemical nature. Yet the Aprista movement does have a fairly detailed program for Peru and a broad program for all Latin America.

The Aprista ideas and program are the product of a long evolutionary process which began with general aspirations expressed in 1924 and was climaxed by a unique theory of history. All the Aprista writers insist that their ideas are simple, yet they do not appear to be so, since, as Carleton Beals has pointed out, these ideas have been labeled "communistic, socialistic, liberal, petty bourgeois, fascist."[2] It is evident that they cannot be all of these at once even if they may resemble one or more of them. The simplest way to describe Aprismo probably is as a distinctive movement which has emerged from the Peruvian social scene.[3]

The Apristas themselves have tried to simplify their ideas by answering in one sentence the question: "What is the Peruvian Aprista party?"

> It is the great movement of the people and of the Peruvian youth, it is the popular coalition of the manual and intellectual workers who have as a patriotic and social ideal a Peru renovated by Justice, by Culture, by Liberty, and by a democratic respect for the rights of all Peruvians to live, to work, to govern themselves, to educate themselves, and to argue, without foreign imperialism or internal tyranny.[4]

---

[1] The best published bibliography is that by Luis Alberto Sánchez and Alfredo M. Saco, "Aprista Bibliography: Books and Pamphlets," *Hispanic American Historical Review,* XXIII (August, 1943), 555–585.

[2] *America South* (1937), pp. 397–398.

[3] "Aprismo is distinguished by being a South American movement, the first truly indigenous and completely formulated system of political and social thought that has appeared in the history of Latin America." From a report by a study group of members of the Royal Institute of International Affairs, *The Republics of South America* (1937), p. 164.

[4] El Buró de Redactores de "Cuaderno Aprista," *40 preguntas y 40 respuestas sobre el Partido Aprista Peruano* (1941), p. 4. The Apristas like to talk of themselves as a

This is a good definition, since its represents Aprismo as a movement for the transformation of Peru into a modern, democratic state. This definition, however, needs much amplification to demonstrate the unique character of the ideas expounded by the Apristas, since they cannot be labeled easily with any of the terms used to describe the political movements of the United States or Western Europe. When someone asked Haya de la Torre[5] whether Aprismo resembled fascism or communism, Haya's answer was that "it does not resemble either one. It resembles our America[6] which you call Latin America and we call Indoamerica. None of the familiar stereotypes that serve to classify the contemporary European tendencies are valid in semi-colonial Latin America. There the economic and political facts, the human type, and the new ideas require a completely new and original terminology. Probably the term 'Aprismo' is itself sufficient."[7] Haya de la Torre's comment, that Aprismo resembles America, lies at the base of the Aprista ideology. Aprismo is an attempt to formulate a program for Latin America based on the situation within that area.[8]

---

great movement, e.g., "the Aprista ideas are not only the ideas of a party. They express and orient the profound sentiments of the great majority of the 130 million Latin Americans." Víctor Raúl Haya de la Torre, *Y después de la guerra ¿qué?* (1946), p. 204.

[5] The Aprista movement is so intimately connected with the life of Haya de la Torre that some critics do not attempt to separate the two. Haya was the founder of the organization; he has been its presidential candidate in Peru; he is the jefe of the organization. But the Aprista movement is much more than a one-man organization; its ranks include many outstanding persons. Both Haya and the Aprista organization have always claimed that he was not the dictator of the organization. Winston Churchill is the official leader of the British Conservative party, yet no one calls that a one-man party. Haya plays a similar role in the Aprista movement. Manuel Seoane writes that "Haya de la Torre is for us a symbol and the incarnation of our program." *Páginas polémicas* (1931), p. 23. Haya himself, takes the same view. "When I think of the exaltation of the name of Haya de la Torre I always think of the chief of our party, a rather ideal symbol and never of myself. Even to me the name of Haya de la Torre is something outside of my own person. I think of him as of the chief and I think of myself as a soldier whose only duty is to be ready to every effort and sacrifice for the party to which I belong. I am conscious of my defects and limitations and I fight every day against them. I know that I am neither a genius nor a saint and that there are in the party many men and women who are superior to me in many ways. But although I know it I think that the faith that so many people have put upon me as a leader may help very much to keep the unity of the Party, and to do the great work that everybody in it must do to achieve our aims. So I extrovert my own personality and I put it to the full service of the common ideal, but never, never as a pedestal for my own vanity." From a letter by Haya quoted in John A. Mackay, *That Other America* (1935), pp. 110–111. See also Luis Alberto Sánchez, *Carta a una indoamericana, cuestiones elementales del aprismo* (1932), pp. 36–37.

[6] Hubert Herring writes in *Good Neighbors* (1941), p. 267, "Aprismo is as indigenous as the llama, born and bred of the Peruvian soil."

[7] In Felipe Cossio del Pomar, *Haya de la Torre, el indoamericano* (1946), p. 149.

[8] One of the slogans which the Apristas use reads, "It is necessary to seek the reality of America, not to invent it." See the inside front covers of Manuel Seoane, *Comunistas criollos* (1933) and Víctor Raúl Haya de la Torre, *Instructiva secreta a V. R. Haya de la Torre* (1933). See also Víctor Raúl Haya de la Torre, *El antimperialismo y el Apra* (1936), p. 167; see Appendix B, p. 134.

Although the Aprista thinkers sought a program applicable to Latin America, they did not turn to the successful revolutionary movement in Mexico for a model. That is not to say that the Mexican revolution did not influence the young Peruvians, because it did. The influence, however, was more inspirational than ideological. The Mexican revolution stimulated the founders of the Aprista movement, but they turned to other sources for their program.

Searching for a program, the young Peruvians seized upon the ideas of European socialism. In the early 1920's the Russian revolution was new and dazzling. From Mexico's revolutionary ferment came much talk about socialism. José Carlos Mariátegui had returned from Europe a convinced and enthusiastic Marxist. As a result of these influences, particularly that of Mariátegui, the Apristas adopted the main conclusions set forth in Marx's philosophy and became Socialists.[9]

As the Apristas understood Marx's philosophy it included four parts: dialectical materialism, the materialistic conception of history, Marxian economics, and the idea that there was a certain evolutionary development in history which proceeds almost despite men's wishes.[10] Of these four the Apristas never made much use of Marxian economics, but the other three were of great importance in the development of their ideas. Dialectical materialism gave them the idea that everything in the world is in a state of flux. The materialistic conception of history impressed upon them the importance of economic factors in the development of society. From their understanding of Marxism also came their view of man. They saw man as the product of his environment who would be superior or inferior, good or bad, better or worse, depending upon how the forces within society affected him.[11]

The Apristas understood that Marx was able to forecast the development of nineteenth-century Europe by applying his materialistic conception of history. They proposed to follow Marx's example and apply his methods to twentieth-century Latin America in order to discover its true character.[12] Marxism taught them that the economic organization of a country determined its social development. Marxism also taught them that the economic basis of society is continually changing and developing. The Marxian dialectic is the tool which helps one to understand this continually changing society. The Apristas proposed to study the organization of society so that political measures could be advocated

[9] Luis Alberto Sánchez, *Aprismo y religión* (1933), p. 22.
[10] Alfredo Saco, *Síntesis Aprista* (1934), p. 34.
[11] Partido Aprista Peruano, *El proceso de Haya de la Torre* (1933), p. lvii.
[12] Haya de la Torre, *El antimperialismo y el Apra*, pp. 117–118.

which would guide the development of Peru in harmony with its true character. The Apristas wanted to remake Peru by guiding this development so that life would become better for the Peruvian people.

Using their understanding of the Marxist method of analysis, the Apristas looked at America. Almost immediately they found they could not combine the Marxian analysis of society with the conditions of life in Peru. Marx talked about the destruction of the capitalist system by the working class which would institute a socialist society. Industrial workers were to be the base of the new society envisioned by Marx. But the young Peruvians who were searching for a program saw no large working class facing a small capitalist class in their country. In fact, they saw very little capitalism.[13] Marxism called imperialism the last stage of capitalism, but the Apristas saw that imperialism within Peru was the creator of industrialism; it was the first stage of capitalism.[14]

Not being able to apply Marxism to the Peruvian social scene the Apristas began to restudy the writings of Marx. In doing so, they discovered that Marx thought all countries would follow a course of economic development similar to England's, from feudalism to capitalism and eventually to socialism. The Apristas were particularly impressed by Marx's idea that the so-called "backward countries" could see their future by looking at England's past. The Apristas looked at Peru and saw that decades after Marx made his prediction reality had not confirmed this idea.[15] Peru was not following in the footsteps of England, but rather developing along a different path. Their attention was thus forced to a study of the actual conditions within Peru, and as they studied their country they became convinced orthodox Marxism was not applicable to it.

At the same time, the Apristas had learned from González Prada, from Mariátegui, and from others to interest themselves in the problem of the Indian. Their interest in the role of the Indian in Peruvian society made them aware that there were two groups in Peru, the Indian element and the Europeanized element, living side by side but not really intermingled. The Indian was outside the economy; he was self-sufficient; in many cases he did not speak Spanish. The Europeanized element was concentrated on the coast and in the cities.

Taking a hint from Marx's idea that a certain evolutionary development in history proceeds almost despite men's wishes, the Apristas hit upon what was to be the key to their thinking. They thought that they

[13] Manuel Seoane, *Nuestros fines* (1931), p. 22.
[14] Víctor Raúl Haya de la Torre, *Espacio-tiempo histórico* (1948), p. 12.
[15] *Ibid.*, pp. 120–121.

could see a fairly orderly development of life in Peru until the arrival of the Spaniards. The conquest seemed to have disrupted indigenous life by introducing ways of doing things foreign to the native people.[16] From this they moved on to wondering if there were not something within Peru which did not fit into the ways of the Spaniards, something "which conspired in favor of its peculiar personality."[17] Turning more and more to a study of history, the Apristas came to the conclusion that the problems of Peru had their base in the fact that ever since the arrival of the Spaniards two antagonistic cultures had been living side by side. The Apristas decided that a program was needed which could merge the two streams of culture, thus opening the road to a new orderly development.[18]

The idea of trying to merge the two cultures existing within Peru is a reflection of a much larger movement, the reawakening of Latin America which came during the 1920's when certain varied currents in world thought combined to inspire thinkers to study conditions in Latin America. Luis Alberto Sánchez, one of the leading Aprista thinkers, connects this reawakening with a new interpretation of the history of America.[19] Sánchez points out that during the last one hundred years the oldest date recognized for the history of America has been pushed back from about A.D. 1000 to a period between 8000 and 15000 B.C. The new consciousness of the antiquity of American civilization had its repercussions in the social field. Latin Americans are a proud people, and they "took pride in their old stock." They began to realize that America was only a new world to the Europeans; it was an old world to history and to Americans whose ancestors had lived in it for a very long time.[20]

As this pride in their ancient lineage appeared, certain other forces began to operate in Latin America. According to Sánchez, these forces included an attempt by Florentino Ameghino to validate the theory of the *homo pampeanus;* the defeat of Spain in 1898 and the rise of the United States, a part of America, to status as a world power; the Mexican revolution and the agitation of the masses which accompanied it;

---

[16] Partido Aprista Peruano, *op. cit.*, pp. 37–38.

[17] *Ibid.*, p. xiii.

[18] Antenor Orrego writes that the realization that the two hostile cultures, which have existed side by side, must be amalgamated is the fundamental characteristic which differentiates his generation from all previous generations. Antenor Orrego, "El sentido vital de la revolución indoamericana," in Saco, *Síntesis Aprista,* p. 11; see also Antenor Orrego, *El pueblo-continente* (1939), pp. 41–44.

[19] Luis Alberto Sánchez, "A New Interpretation of the History of America," *Hispanic American Historical Review,* XXIII (August, 1943), 441–456.

[20] *Ibid.*, p. 442.

the commemoration of the first centenary of independence in many American republics; and, finally, the First World War and its aftereffects, the Russian revolution and the rise of new movements in Germany and Italy. The most important of these forces was probably Europe's loss of glamour and prestige for the Latin Americans, but all contributed to the creation of a historic consciousness within Latin America. Sánchez points out that this intellectual ferment had its repercussions in the historical, economic, and political fields. It led Latin American thinkers to turn their attention to their native soil and to take an interest in the problem of the unassimilated Indian population.[21]

The new interpretation of history included an awareness of the dual character of history in Latin America which combined an indigenous element and a Europeanized creole or mestizo element; an anti-European trend; an agrarian and socializing influence; and an anti-imperialistic outlook. According to Sánchez, the Aprista movement is the most authentic and concrete expression of this new outlook on the history of Latin America.[22]

It is no accident that the Apristas were part of the current of reinterpretation of American history. Most leaders of this movement were not born in Lima, which is the most Europeanized city of Peru. Many of them were born in Trujillo, near the ruins of the ancient city of Chan-Chan, once the center of the empire of the Chimú. Other Apristas were born in Cuzco and other highland cities where signs of the Inca presence were everywhere. The Indian heritage of Peru was thus early impressed upon future leaders of the Aprista movement.

As has been mentioned, Sánchez points out that the political expression of the new historical consciousness in Latin America is represented by the Apristas. This was first expressed in 1924 when the five basic principles of the movement were set down by Víctor Raúl Haya de la Torre. The five fundamental propositions were: "anti-imperialism, the nationalization of land and industries, the internationalization of the Panama Canal, the economic and political unity of Latin America, and solidarity with the oppressed peoples of the earth."[23] All these propositions imply a fundamentally different concept of the role of Latin America in contemporary history. According to Sánchez, the new ideas flowed out of the fact that the new interpretation of the history of America stimulated interest in two facets of Latin American life which had been greatly neglected until then: the revaluation of the role of

[21] *Ibid.*, pp. 442–443.
[22] *Ibid.*, pp. 443–444.
[23] *Ibid.*, p. 444.

the Indian and the interest in economics which was also stimulated by the interest in Marxism. With these two present, Latin America could no longer be looked upon as merely European in its culture, and its history could no longer be looked upon as only political and military.[24]

The interest in the true character of Latin America led the Apristas to attack what they called the intellectual colonialism of so many Latin Americans, the habit of continually looking toward Europe for ideas. This, too, is a reflection of what Sánchez calls Latin America's attainment of political maturity.[25] The new maturity rejected the European model; because America was different from Europe it needed a different method of organizing its life. The Apristas propose that Latin America work out its problems on the basis of conditions within the area. They sum this up in a pithy slogan which states that they seek "the mental emancipation of Indoamerica from the patterns and dictates of Europe."[26]

Because of their emphasis upon looking realistically at Latin America, the Apristas spent much energy discussing what name should be given to the area south of the Rio Grande. They look upon this area as a homogeneous entity and they give it the name Indoamerica. This name, they say, is truly descriptive of the area, for it takes account of the two parts contained therein: the indigenous, the aboriginal, all that was present before 1492, and the European contribution. The name Indoamerica does not apply to Canada and the United States, they say, because there the Europeans destroyed the native element. The Apristas object to all the old names given to their Indoamerica. Hispanic America they do not like because it goes with the idea of the viceroyalty. Latin America, they say, is a French invention which came into use during the nineteenth century as part of the anti-Spanish sentiment of that period. The Apristas do not like the use of the term because it is too European and excludes the millions of people in the area who are not Latins, but are Indians, Negroes, and the descendants of the British, Germans, Chinese, and Japanese. Spanish America is a colonial reminder, and its use ignores Brazil and Haiti which are not Spanish in any sense. Pan America, the Apristas believe, is connected with the idea of dollar diplomacy and includes the whole continent without distinguishing its two essential parts. They are for the use of Indoamerica.[27]

[24] *Ibid.*, p. 446.

[25] *Ibid.*, p. 454.

[26] Haya de la Torre, *Espacio-tiempo histórico*, p. 15; Luis Alberto Sánchez, *Raúl Haya de la Torre o el político* (1934), pp. 107, 123.

[27] Sánchez, "A New Interpretation of the History of America," pp. 445–446; Víctor Raúl Haya de la Torre, "El significado político del nombre," and "Cuestión de nom-

The point they emphasize is that the use of this name leads to a clearer understanding of the area. Indoamerica suggests the two component parts of the area, and use of the term, the Apristas insist, would prevent exclusive concentration upon the needs of the Europeanized section of the population.

As a corollary to their use of the name Indoamerica, the Apristas make a determined effort to interest their followers in the past glories of the Inca Empire[28] and the conditions of life of the Peruvian Indian. History is important in order to understand politics; hence the young Apristas are urged to study history and the lessons to be learned from its course. As an Aprista pamphlet puts it, "With the history of Peru in their hand, the young Apristas struggle to correct the errors of the past."[29]

In spite of the Aprista emphasis upon America, the Aprista leaders originally adopted European Marxism and tried to develop a Socialist program for America. As a result, the Aprista writings contain many quotations from Marx, Engels, Lenin, and other writers who called themselves Socialists. The Aprista writings use the words socialist and socialism a great deal. The Apristas do not, however, call their movement Socialist for many reasons. They look upon the Marxian philosophy as a tool, a method, and not as a bible which must be religiously followed. They point out that the word socialism is a very confusing term. It has had many meanings and there are various kinds of Socialists: Christian, guild, libertarian, Marxian, reformist, agrarian, and many other kinds. Aprismo is none of these things, but a combination of socialism and the reality of Latin America. Just as they understand Bolshevism or Marxism-Leninism to be a combination of Marxian socialism and Russian reality, so Aprismo or Marxism-Aprismo is a combination of Marxian socialism and the reality of America.[30] If the Apristas represent a school of Socialist thought, they certainly are not orthodox.

bres," *¿A dónde va Indoamérica?* (1935), pp. 21–35; Víctor Raúl Haya de la Torre, "¡No nos avergoncemos de llamarnos indoamericanos!," *La defensa continental* (1942), pp. 69–90.

[28] The Aprista almanac begins its list of the governments of Peru with Manco Cápac, 1067–1107, who was the first Inca, and ends with José Luis Bustamante y Rivero, who was President at the time the almanac was published. *Almanaque la tribuna 1948*, pp. 89–92. In 1942, the Aprista party convention decided to celebrate the 29th of August as the "Day of the Inca Empire and of the Indian." They picked this day because it was the anniversary of the death of the last Inca ruler. *Resoluciones de la convención de dirigentes del Partido Aprista Peruano, reunida en Lima, Perú, 1942* (1942), p. 11.

[29] El Buró de Redactores de "Cuaderno Aprista," *op. cit.*, p. 22.

[30] Alfredo Saco and G. Vegas León, "Por qué aprismo y no socialismo," *¡Partidos de frente único para Indoamérica!* (1938), pp. 8–9.

The Historical Space-Time Theory

After years of discussion of the differences between Europe and Latin America the ideas of the Apristas on this subject became crystallized into a new theory of history, the theory of historical space-time. The theory had its origin in the contradiction—apparent to the Aprista leaders—between the evidence offered by the ruins of ancient civilizations to be seen in Peru and the historic chronology taught in the Peruvian schools which made A.D. 1492 the date when American history began. What troubled the Apristas was that the "New World" was apparently as old as the Old World of Europe. They looked at the ruins of Chan-Chan and wondered how they could be called new when the eye disclosed their apparent antiquity. This doubt about the place of America in world history remained in the back of Haya de la Torre's mind for many years. When the new ideas of relativity in the physical sciences became known, Haya thought he could see a connection between the new interpretations of the physical sciences and history. Taking ideas from a series of writers including Einstein, Hegel, Toynbee, Spengler, and from life, Haya combined them into the theory of historical space-time.[31]

According to Haya de la Torre, the theory of historical space-time is only relativity applied to history and is an outgrowth of the Marxian interpretation of history.[32] Aprismo developed out of Marxian philosophy from which it learned the use of the dialectic. The dialectic principle holds that contradictions are inherent in all things. If this is true, then contradictions exist within Marxism which will eventually lead to its displacement by a new philosophy of history. Marxism was based on an understanding of the world derived from the concepts of time and space held during the nineteenth century. Using this understanding, Marx was able to build up his theory.[33]

The process of the world's development, according to Haya, did not stop with Marx. Our century is merely a link in a chain of development leading from the forgotten past into the unforeseen future. Influenced by all the collected knowledge of the past, the world today is living through a revolution in scientific thinking which is changing our concepts of space and time. Haya de la Torre writes, "The revolution which

[31] The theory is set forth in Víctor Raúl Haya de la Torre, *Espacio-tiempo histórico* (1948). Haya became interested in the theory of relativity in 1930 when he met Einstein in Berlin. See "Un discurso de Einstein," *Ex-combatientes y desocupados* (1936), pp. 228–233.

[32] Haya de la Torre, *Espacio-tiempo histórico*, pp. 21–22.

[33] *Ibid.*, pp. 3–7.

the world is passing through is not only economic, social, and political. It is a cultural and technical revolution, and more important than that, it is a radical cosmological revolution. That is to say, this revolution embraces the very foundations of human knowledge, for it brings the negation of the great scientific truths, held unimpeachable till now, upon which we have erected our conception of the world, of nature, of the cosmos, of time, and of space."[34] Does this revolution apply to the social sciences? Haya de la Torre answers this question in the affirmative. He states that the concepts of space, time, motion, matter, and gravitation held at any period are the bases upon which philosophies are developed. In other words, all interpretations of history are based on the general scientific concepts in vogue at the time. Haya de la Torre states that the discoveries of Galileo, Kepler, and Newton were followed by the appearance of new philosophies. Hegel, Kant, Marx, all based their philosophies upon Newtonian physics. In our epoch the new ideas of physics developed by Einstein and others are changing all our concepts about time, matter, and energy. Therefore, writes Haya, we must include this new interpretation in our philosophy of history.[35]

The new concept presented by the discoveries of physics defines a new fourth dimension called space-time. In this concept space in itself and time in itself have both collapsed into a kind of union that permits them to preserve an independent existence. The new space-time of the physicists, according to the Apristas, must be incorporated into a philosophy of history if that philosophy is to give a true picture of the contemporary world.[36]

Haya de la Torre states that "there is no absolute time nor any absolute space, as was thought until Einstein's scientific revolution. This is the scientific principle which now permits us to observe the historic process, not as a single process, but as many processes which offer different perspectives."[37] In the theory of historical space-time, therefore, history is interpreted "as a vast universal co-ordination of processes, each one inseparable from its own space-time and motion."[38] It must be noted that the words space and time as used in the phrase historical space-time do not carry the old meanings of the words, but rather space-time in a new relativist sense. History is created by "the vital interdependency of telluric, ethnic, social, economic, cultural, and psychological factors which act and are influenced by each other and

[34] *Ibid.*, p. 87.
[35] *Ibid.*, pp. 88–100.
[36] *Ibid.*, p. 8.
[37] *Ibid.*, p. 124.
[38] *Ibid.*, p. 21.

include a dynamic continuum which constitutes a philosophic category which can be named the fourth dimension of history."[39] This new dimension is historical space-time.

If it is remembered that, according to Haya de la Torre, historic space and historic time are inseparable and, therefore, must be expressed in a single term, historical space-time, a definition of historic space and historic time as used in this theory can be attempted. Historic space is the scene in which the life of the people develops. It is not geography, although that is included, but rather the total of man, earth, tradition, ethnic composition, and the interrelation of these with what is called soul or conscience, or spirit of a people. Historic space is the peculiar combination that gives us the entire social scene.[40] Historic time is the stage of a people's development, economically, politically, culturally, as determined by the forms of production and by the social development that motivates or influences them. Historic time is also the feeling and the expression of social time which flows from all of the relations between man as a part of a community and his historic space which determine the level of man's cultural consciousness. This feeling for time can be seen by comparing the idea of time held by an industrial worker in the United States and an Andean Indian. Each has a completely different conception.[41] These two, historic space and historic time, are inseparable and they combine to create historical space-time which includes everything that affects the life of a social group.[42]

Thus in each historical space-time a multiplicity of factors work to create the consciousness of the area. Space-time is not the simple addition of all the factors involved, but these and something more which flows from the spirit of the people. Haya gives the example of Greece and points out that all of the physical factors which made Greece great are present today, yet the people who inhabit the area now cannot combine them to bring back the glory of ancient Greece.[43] He also points out that people in different areas have the same desires, but they may satisfy them in different ways. The difference is the space-time factor.[44] Each historical space-time is a rather large area. According to this theory, the world is not divided into continents, but into various continental peoples. China, Russia, Western Europe, the United States, and Indoamerica, among others, are the homes of continental peoples.[45]

---

[39] *Loc. cit.*

[40] *Ibid.*, pp. 32, 58; El Buró de Redactores de "Cuaderno Aprista," *La verdad del aprismo* (1940), pp. 1–2.

[41] Haya de la Torre, *Espacio-tiempo histórico*, pp. 32–33, 58.

[42] *Ibid.*, pp. 58–59.

[43] *Ibid.*, p. 65.

[44] *Ibid.*, pp. 26–27.

[45] *Ibid.*, pp. 34–35.

From the theory of historical space-time the Apristas conclude that the social development of each continental people is relative and determined by historical space-time. In history, therefore, the concept of a single universal scheme is no longer valid.[46] Capitalism has taken different forms of development in various places demonstrating that "history is not a single process but a series of processes."[47] At this point the Apristas differentiate themselves from orthodox Marxism. They claim that Marx described an orderly system of world history in which the process began in antiquity and would inevitably culminate in the era of the proletariat. This view of history, according to the Apristas, is completely out of harmony with reality. They claim that Marx's ideas were the product of his epoch and not eternal truths.[48] Marx's inevitable development of society toward a proletarian world, the Apristas claim, may have been good reasoning in nineteenth-century Europe, but is passé for twentieth-century Latin America.

Because of this attempt by the Apristas to adapt Marxism to the reality of Latin America, the apparatus of the international Communist movement has continually fought the Aprista movement.[49] The Communists claim that their version of Marxism answers all questions and applies to all countries and, therefore, organizations like the Aprista movement are unnecessary.[50] As the Communists put it, "The theoretical assertion made by the Apristas that the rule of Marxism-Leninism is not applicable to Latin-America is a falsehood of complete falseness *(falsa de toda falsedad).*"[51]

The Apristas deny this claim made by the Communists. They maintain there can be no parallelism in the development of peoples just as there is no parallelism in the new physics. The Apristas, therefore, come to the conclusion that Latin America cannot have the same kind of economic development as that through which Europe passed.[52] It must follow a course of development in harmony with its own character.

[46] *Ibid.*, p. 25.
[47] *Ibid.*, p. 121.
[48] *Ibid.*, p. 23.
[49] The Communist writings on Aprismo include R. E. Martínez de la Torre, *Páginas anti-Apristas, apuntes para una interpretación marxista de historia social del Perú* (1933); Juan Vargas, *Aprismo y marxismo* (1936); Julio Antonio Mella, *La lucha contra el imperialismo, qué es el Arpa?* [*sic*] (1928); Cesar A. Guardia Mayorga, *Reconstruyendo el aprismo. Exposición y crítica de la doctrina política y filosófica hayista* (1945).
[50] This is the issue which divided Tito and Stalin. The Yugoslav Communists claim that there is no one formula for establishing a socialist society; therefore, methods to be employed in converting any country to socialism must take into account its history, traditions, and peculiar conditions.
[51] Vargas, *op. cit.*, p. 13.
[52] Haya de la Torre, *Espacio-tiempo histórico*, p. 12.

Manuel Seoane points out that traveling across Peru is almost the equivalent of a trip in H. G. Wells's time machine.[53] In Peru, Indians who have never used the wheel look up to see airplanes flying over their homes. Haya de la Torre points out that the Arabs were in Spain twice as long as the Spaniards were in Peru, yet Spain did not become an Arabic country although it assimilated certain features from Arabic culture. In the same way, he maintains, Peru eventually will develop a true Peruvian civilization which will include features taken from the Spaniards yet remain Peruvian. This demonstrates, to the Apristas, the impossibility of the development of Peru paralleling the course of Europe in the past. Most of Peru's problems, say the Apristas, originate in the attempts by its governments to follow European patterns which cannot be fitted into the Peruvian social scene.[54]

A second conclusion drawn by the Apristas from the historical space-time theory is that the angle from which any phenomenon is observed helps to explain what one sees. This has been demonstrated in the physical laboratory and is also true with historical phenomena. The history of the world seen from Indoamerica will look different than when seen from Europe. Therefore, Haya de la Torre contends, there can be no universal scheme in history valid for all the world where history can be neatly divided into ancient times, the middle ages, and modern times. If one uses this threefold division there is no place for the pre-Columbian cultures of America or for the Hindu, the Chinese, and the Australian aboriginal cultures.[55] In practical political thinking, this emphasis upon the unique character of Indoamerica leads the Aprista movement to seek new formulas for the solution of its problems.

The Aprista Interpretation of Peruvian History

Using the theory of historical space-time the Apristas have worked out an interpretation of the history of Peru which they use as a base for their program.[56] In this interpretation the history of Peru begins during the time when migratory tribes first began to wander over America. When the tribes settled down, civilization began to develop. Just as in

[53] Seoane, *Nuestros fines,* p. 23.

[54] Haya de la Torre, *¿A dónde va Indoamérica?,* pp. 23–25; Seoane, *Comunistas criollos,* pp. 24–25.

[55] Haya de la Torre, *Espaciotiempo histórico,* pp. 12, 16–18.

[56] The Aprista interpretation of the history of Latin America is scattered through their writings. For systematic historic interpretation, see: Luis Alberto Sánchez, *Los fundamentos de la historia de América* (1943); Sánchez, *Carta a una indoamericana,* pp. 4–13; Víctor Raúl Haya de la Torre, *Teoría y táctica del aprismo* (1931), pp. 5–16; Haya de la Torre, *El antimperialismo y el Apra,* pp. 167–183; Partido Aprista Peruano, *El proceso Haya de la Torre,* pp. ix–xvii.

all societies, a constant process of change and development took place which was fairly orderly and culminated in the Inca Empire.

The Spaniards broke the orderly rhythm of development. But they did something more which was to have tremendous importance in the further course of events. They introduced new ways of doing things but failed to destroy the old. Rather, both the old and the new lived on side by side. The most striking example was the system of landholding. The Spaniards created the latifundium, a form of private property, alongside of the *ayllu,* the primitive collectivism of the Inca culture. At the same time, race mixture produced the mestizo, and the occupation created the creole. To complicate the population picture still further, the Spaniards brought Negro slaves into Peru. The gap between the old culture and the new was accentuated when Pizarro turned his back on the native centers of population and created a new city, Lima, as the center from which to dominate the country.

During colonial days the creole group developed into a rich and powerful class which became restless under the Spanish monopoly of political and economic power. The creoles wanted freedom from Spain, in particular, freedom to carry on trade with non-Spanish groups. Using the ideology of the French revolution, the creoles fostered the American revolution. This introduced a new paradox into Peru, for, whereas in France the revolutionaries used the new ideas to destroy the latifundia, in Peru the same phraseology was used to uphold the latifundia. After independence all went on as before except that the direct influence of Spain was removed. The colonial spirit lived on in the new republic because "the revolution for independence only brought the emancipation of one class: the creole feudal class. The others, the middle class, the rural classes, and the emerging proletariat, had only won a simple change of lord and master."[57]

After independence Peru remained predominantly agricultural, and its small industries could not supply the growing needs of the population. Hence began the development of Peru as a market for foreign manufactured goods. At the same time, Peru became a source of supply for raw materials for the growing industries of the United States and Western Europe. This led to the growth of imperialism, which introduced another social system into Peru.

Today Peru has within it, therefore, a whole series of social systems. The fairly orderly development which took place in Western Europe and the United States from feudalism to mercantilism to capitalism

[57] Partido Aprista Peruano, *op. cit.,* p. xv.

climaxed by intense industrialization and imperialism never occurred in Peru. Living within Peru are primitive jungle peoples, some of whom are cannibals; the barbaric Indians, whose progress toward civilization under the Incas was halted by the Spaniards; feudal landowners with fifteenth-century mentalities; and the people of the coastal cities with a European outlook. Each of these groups lives its life scarcely touched by the actions of the other groups. The state in Peru reflects this peculiar social reality. The rich control the state by using violence and by taking advantage of ignorance to remain in power. Power fluctuates among the landowners, the agents of foreign capital, and the militarists.

As a result of this interpretation of Peruvian history, the Apristas come to the conclusion that the problems of Peru and of Latin America are unique. To solve these problems, they believe that it is necessary to study Peru thoroughly and on the basis of the facts to use state power to create a situation in which all the varied forces within the country can harmoniously coöperate. The failure of the conquest and the republic to develop a stable progressive civilization merely confirms this need to them.

Both Peru and Latin America, the Apristas maintain, need to find a completely new system of governmental and economic organization. The European system cannot work in Indoamerica. Europe's great problem is limited space and overpopulation, and hence a need for overseas colonies. Indoamerica is underpopulated, underdeveloped, and rich in natural resources. It must find a method of developing its resources, increasing its population, and creating a stable society which is able to develop in harmony with its true character. The Apristas propose to find this program, build up an organization which will capture state power, and help to create the Peru and Indoamerica of tomorrow.[58]

A Program for Latin America

Searching for the reality within Latin America led the Apristas to construct a program which, they believe, if put into practice would result in the creation of a democratic and powerful United States of Latin America. The program can be divided into two parts, one for all of Latin America, called the maximum program, and one for Peru, called the minimum program. Because the Apristas look upon Latin America as a unit, they believe that the fundamental problems facing the twenty republics can be solved by the adoption of the Aprista maximum program.[59] The maximum program is an ideal toward which all Aprista

[58] Haya de la Torre, *Y después de la guerra ¿qué?*, p. 242.
[59] Víctor Raúl Haya de la Torre, *Política Aprista* (1933), p. 96.

activity is aimed, a goal which will be attained only after a long process of education and development.[60] It has as its main purpose the creation of a situation where the people of Latin America can be themselves (*ser nosotros mismos*).[61] To this end the Apristas think that Latin America needs liberty; and to achieve this aim they put forward their solution: to achieve true independence it is necessary to control imperialistic penetration of the area, to strengthen the area by uniting it politically and economically, and to nationalize the wealth of Latin America.

ANTI-IMPERIALISM

Action against imperialism is the first plank of the Aprista maximum program.[62] This comes first because the Apristas believe that the most important problem facing Latin America is that created by imperialistic penetration within the area. The Apristas come to this conclusion from studying history, which, they say, teaches them that foreign interests, in coöperation with certain of the ruling groups of the twenty republics, have been slowly taking over all the important wealth of the area. The Apristas have learned, according to Luis Alberto Sánchez, that "the governing classes in Latin America favored imperialism and opposed education so the people would remain ignorant and not know the economic fundamentals of political life. [Then the governing classes] mortgaged the national wealth of the continent in order to maintain themselves in, and in order to be able to enjoy power."[63] As a result of this opinion the Apristas think that "each and every one of the nations of the Indoamerican continent is in danger of being subjugated economically and politically by imperialism."[64] The Apristas view imperialism as a world phenomenon, but think it plays a more important role in Latin America than in any other part of the world.[65]

The Apristas define imperialism as an economic phenomenon. They view it as the expansion of forces within one country into another. They think this outward expansion is inevitable in a highly industrialized country based on the capitalist system of production. As the Apristas

[60] El Buró de Redactores de "Cuaderno Aprista," *La verdad del aprismo* (1940), pp. 7–8.

[61] Partido Aprista Peruano, *El proceso Haya de la Torre*, p. xlv.

[62] The Aprista writings on this subject include: Víctor Raúl Haya de la Torre, *El antimperialismo y el Apra* (1936); Carlos Manuel Cox, *En torno al imperialismo* (1933); Alberto Daniel Faleroni, *Frente único antiimperialista* (1938) (Faleroni is an Argentine Aprista); Fernando León de Vivero, *Avance del imperialismo fascista en el Perú* (1938); Pedro Muñiz, *Penetración imperialista* (1935); Manuel Seoane. *La garra yanqui* (1930).

[63] Sánchez, *Carta a una indoamericana*, p. 9.

[64] Saco, *Síntesis Aprista*, p. 55.

[65] Orrego, *El pueblo-continente*, p. 127.

see the process, capitalism forces an industrially developed country to seek raw materials in the underdeveloped areas of the world. At the same time, an industrial country must seek markets for the manufactured goods which cannot be consumed at home. Imperialism, to the Apristas, "is a historic-economic phenomenon inherent in the industrial system of our epoch."[66] The outward expansion of the industrial countries is fostered by their governments, according to the Apristas who believe these governments use their economic and political power to aid the private interests which are entering underdeveloped nations.[67] Basing their theory upon this belief, the Apristas maintain that the weak, underdeveloped countries must inevitably fall before the onslaught of the powerful, industrial countries unless they can find the strength to resist this pressure.

The world today appears to be an economic unit to the Apristas. In this economically unified world, the republics of Latin America are economic dependencies of the world capitalist system, the centers of which are located in the United States and Western Europe.[68] Because they are dependencies, the Apristas maintain that the imperialist countries control Latin American production, manage its finances, set the value to its currency, set the prices on Latin American products, and regulate the salary level in the area. The Apristas argue that in this system the interests of the imperialist country and the imperialist enterprise are considered most important. Whatever benefits Latin America receives are merely incidental, secondary to the interests of the imperialists. What is more important to the Apristas, the imperialist influence moves from economic affairs into Latin American politics, and governments become subservient to foreign interests.[69]

The Apristas understand that capitalist production is a higher form of production than feudalism, higher in the sense that it produces more commodities at a cheaper price. They welcome the entrance of foreign capital into Latin America, therefore, recognizing that it performs a necessary and useful role in the economic life of the area. They concede that "Indoamerica has been enriched and been able to begin its development toward capitalism thanks to the arrival of imperialist capital."[70] The Apristas point out, however, that foreign capital does more than merely enrich a country and stimulate its development toward capitalism; it also disrupts and disorganizes the native economy. That is the

[66] Haya de la Torre, *Política Aprista*, p. 99.
[67] *Ibid.*, p. 45.
[68] Haya de la Torre, *El antimperialismo y el Apra*, p. 18.
[69] *Ibid.*, pp. 9–20.
[70] Sánchez, *Carta a una indoamericana*, p. 17.

main reason the Apristas are opposed to imperialism. Imperialism, as they define the term, is foreign capital coming to a country in an improper manner.[71] As they see the process, the imperialists come to Latin America not to build up the countries but to make profits. They do not set up many manufacturing plants, but prefer to organize enterprises which produce raw materials or partially make articles which are needed by the industry of the imperialist country. It is the needs of the great imperialist enterprises which are served, not the needs of the people of Latin America.[72]

This situation is complicated still further, according to the Apristas, because imperialist powers and governments of Latin America coöperate to stir up false nationalism within the twenty countries which promotes conflicts: Peru against Chile; Brazil against Argentina; Colombia and Ecuador against Peru; and many others.[73] The Apristas see the imperialist danger growing until the prospect of the complete economic and political subjugation of Latin America is imminent. They point to the fact that foreign investments in Latin America continue to grow until they have reached astronomical figures.[74]

During the early days of the Aprista movement, the Aprista leaders aimed their main fire at United States imperialism although they opposed all imperialism. They believed that the actions of the United States during the first third of this century in Mexico, Nicaragua, Haiti, Cuba, Panama, and the Dominican Republic demonstrated the need for a more vigorous resistance to United States imperialism on the part of Latin America. Originally the Apristas used the phrase "Action against Yankee imperialism" in their propaganda, but they changed this to "Action against imperialism" some time after the Aprista organization was created.[75] Haya de la Torre explained the change by saying that

[71] Felipe Cossio del Pomar, *Haya de la Torre, el indoamericano* (1946), p. 114.

[72] Haya de la Torre, *El antimperialismo y el Apra,* p. 21.

[73] *Ibid.*, pp. 35–36.

[74] *Ibid.*, pp. 37–40.

[75] See *ibid.*, p. 33, n. 2. This change has even made some Apristas change the original slogan, consciously or unconsciously. In Cossio del Pomar's book, *Haya de la Torre, el indoamericano,* the 1924 program reads "Action against imperialism." But in many other places the original slogan is given as "Action against Yankee imperialism"; e.g., Luis Alberto Sánchez, *Raúl Haya de la Torre o el político* (1934), p. 109; Haya de la Torre, *El antimperialismo y el Apra,* p. 33; Haya de la Torre, *Por la emancipación de la América Latina* (1927), p. 188. The change can also be seen in the periodical *Apra* which was published in Mexico during the 1930's. The five-point maximum program was printed as part of the masthead. In the January, 1935 issue, point one of the program reads, "*Acción contra el imperialismo Yanqui.*" The May, 1935, issue reads "*Acción contra el imperialismo.*" Despite the change, this issue contains a half-page cartoon showing a large snake labeled *Imperialismo Yanqui* swallowing Cuba.

when the Aprista organization was created in 1924, in Mexico, it was United States imperialism which was most evident there. When the Apristas popularized the slogan "Against Yankee imperialism" the Communists accused them of being agents of British imperialism. To demonstrate that the Communists were liars and to make their anti-imperialism clearer, the Apristas changed the slogan to omit the word Yankee.[76]

It must be remembered that the Apristas created their organization in the years when the United States followed the policy which Professor Bemis called trying "to convince Latin America that the Big Stick did not really mean imperialism."[77] These were the years when United States Marines were fighting in Nicaragua and the Apristas were supporting Sandino's army.[78] In 1924 Haya de la Torre wrote an article entitled "Is the United States Feared in South America?" and came to the conclusion that it was.[79]

Yet the leaders of the Aprista movement never became bitter toward the United States. Imperialism, to them, was an economic phenomenon. They opposed imperialism in all its manifestations, no matter what its source, but they stated that they did not favor a national or racist conflict with the people of the imperialist nations. They saw the conflict as an economic battle which could not be fought on racial grounds.[80] Haya de la Torre quotes the Declaration of Principles of the Costa Rican section of Apra as the true sentiment of the Aprista program: "The anti-imperialist cause of Apra does not assume a nationalist struggle against the North-American people, but rather a struggle against the economic, political, and social system under which it is conquering, and in whose name the most flagrant violations of the rights of the weak peoples are being committed."[81]

Although the Apristas oppose imperialism, they are not opposed to the entrance of all foreign capital into Latin America. They make a distinction between foreign capital and foreign imperialism. Foreign

---

[76] Haya de la Torre, *El antimperialismo y el Apra*, p. 197.

[77] Samuel Flagg Bemis, *The Latin American Policy of the United States* (1943), p. 203.

[78] Haya de la Torre wrote to Froilán Turcios on February 5, 1928, "Since we are soldiers of Apra, we have followed the course of the struggle since the first moment. But believing that it is necessary to give our support more reality, the Peruvian exiles have decided to offer to General Sandino, through you, our contribution of blood for our anti-imperialist campaigns. We are contributing our services unconditionally and putting them at the command of the Nicaraguan Liberating army in order to struggle in its ranks." *¿A dónde va Indoamérica?* (1935), p. 7.

[79] In *The Nation*, vol. 118 (April 9, 1924), 410.

[80] Víctor Raúl Haya de la Torre, *Construyendo el aprismo* (1933), pp. 123–124.

[81] *Ibid.*, pp. 124–125.

capital, the Apristas argue, is essential for the development of the resources of Latin America. This capital should be protected by the laws of the countries to which it comes, for it can play an important role. To the Apristas, there is another kind of foreign capital, that which interferes in internal politics and looks to a foreign country for aid when it comes into conflict with the Latin American people or their governments. This is imperialism, the improper action of foreign capital.[82] The Apristas often compare foreign capital to a river, pointing out that a river can do good or harm. When a river is controlled it helps to cultivate the fields. When it is not controlled it may flood and destroy the fields. In the same way, foreign capital would be good for Latin America if it were controlled, but becomes evil when it is permitted to do as it pleases.[83]

The Apristas assert that they are not interested in fighting the people of the United States or of any other imperialistic country. They claim that they are neither antiforeign nor racist. Their anti-imperialistic struggle is against the trusts of "Wall Street" and of "the City." They maintain that there are millions of people in the "imperialistic" countries who, if they only knew what was happening in Latin America, would be at the side of the Apristas fighting the common enemy. The Apristas also oppose the violent expulsion of foreign capital. They merely want to see it controlled and made to play a role that would benefit the people of the countries of Latin America.[84]

The Apristas have never tried to gain cheap popularity by pointing to a foreign enemy. They maintain that since Latin America needs industrial equipment to build up its economy and since the United States and other industrialized nations need raw materials to keep their economy going, a mutually satisfactory exchange could be worked out if only the drive for quick profits on the side of the imperialist powers and the desire to preserve the status quo on the side of the Latin American ruling groups were halted.[85]

Because of advocating coöperation between the United States and Latin America, the Apristas have been accused of being agents of United States capitalism within Peru. A good example of this charge is seen in a pamphlet published by a trade union, apparently controlled by the Peruvian Communists, which states that "Apra, and with it all of

[82] Haya de la Torre, *Y después de la guerra, ¿qué?*, p. 200.
[83] Cossio del Pomar, *op. cit.*, pp. 114–115; Seoane, *Páginas polémicas*, pp. 35–36.
[84] Cossio del Pomar, *op. cit.*, p. 115; Haya de la Torre, *Y después de la guerra, ¿qué?*, pp. 201–202.
[85] Haya de la Torre, *¿A dónde va Indoamérica?*, pp. 258–259.

its followers, blinded by ambition and the most vulgar opportunism, wishes to surrender the working class of Peru, tied hand and foot, to Apra's friends the imperialists."[86] Charges of this type were common during the period from 1945 to 1948 when the Apristas wished Peru to come to an understanding with its foreign bondholders and make a start on paying off its foreign debt. The Apristas were practical in their arguments. They claimed Peru was forced to look to foreign capital for the development of its economy. The Apristas maintained that the only way to get capital to flow into Peru was to pay off the outstanding debt and so get into good standing with the sources of further borrowing.[87]

Despite what is said of them, the evidence warrants the conclusion that the Apristas oppose imperialism as they interpret the term. They are realists and, knowing that geography has bound the world together, advocate that the industrialized nations and the Latin American raw-material-producing nations find a method of coöperation fair to both. Realizing Peru's need for capital, they do not oppose foreign capital in itself, but rather the harmful effects it produces at times.

FOR THE UNIFICATION OF LATIN AMERICA

Having determined that imperialist penetration was the great enemy of Latin America, the Apristas sought a force capable of opposing this powerful enemy. They came to the conclusion that no force outside Latin America would help it, but that it would have to depend upon its own resources.[88] The Apristas saw only two alternatives facing the area: it could either organize itself for a struggle with imperialism or be doomed to a semicolonial existence.[89] The Apristas, believing that in union there is strength,[90] decided that the way for Latin America to organize for the struggle was to unify itself politically and economically. Unification of Latin America became the second goal of the Aprista maximum program.[91] The Apristas see the need for unification as a logical outcome of their opposition to imperialism. Their argument is

[86] *Conclusiones y resoluciones de la Primera Conferencia Obrera Regional del Sur* (1947), p. 2.

[87] Carlos Manuel Cox, *Dinámica económica del aprismo* (1948), pp. 59–81; Haya de la Torre, *Y después de la guerra ¿qué?*, pp. 65–71.

[88] Haya de la Torre, *El antimperialismo y el Apra*, p. 102; one of the Aprista slogans reads: "The liberation of the people of Latin America will be the work of the Latin American people themselves." Esteban Pavletich, "Mentira sistemática," *Indoamérica*, vol. 1 (August, 1928), 14.

[89] Haya de la Torre, *¿A dónde va Indoamérica?*, pp. 260–261.

[90] Víctor Raúl Haya de la Torre, *La defensa continental* (1942), p. 34.

[91] This is one of the Apristas' oldest conceptions. Haya de la Torre was writing about uniting Latin America in 1923, before Apra was founded. See his *Por la emancipación de América Latina*, p. 29.

that imperialism is strong and the individual republics in Latin America are weak. The twenty republics must, therefore, unite, for "if they do not make themselves strong by uniting they will become colonies like Africa or Oceania."[92]

The Apristas view Latin America as a natural unit which has been divided into twenty states.[93] They look at the present boundary lines between the various republics as arbitrary lines which are a reflection of the Spanish colonial subdivisions, having no real economic justification at this time. The Spaniards based their boundary lines on a feudal system of landholding; therefore, the Apristas maintain, these lines merely help to preserve feudalism without serving any useful purpose.[94]

To the Apristas, the people of Latin America are so similar to one another that they should not be divided into twenty different varieties. Antenor Orrego writes that "from north to south the people have the same rhythm and the same essential emphasis."[95] He compares Latin America to Europe and comes to the conclusion that the boundary lines between the twenty Latin American republics are completely useless. He points out that in Europe the boundary lines are to a certain extent natural: they separate different kinds of people. These peoples built their states at a time when the construction of a national state was a great, progressive step forward. In Latin America, he continues, the boundary lines simply serve to divide people who are basically the same. Orrego characterizes the Latin Americans as a continental people and, therefore, he maintains, their patriotism should be continental and their nationalism should be continental. This continent is, of course, everything from the Rio Grande to the Strait of Magellan.[96]

Regarding Latin America as a unit, the Apristas think it is foolish for political leaders of the area to treat the twenty republics as if each were an island separated from its neighbors by a wide sea.[97] They do not think there is a distinctly Ecuadoran problem, or Peruvian problem, or a special problem involving any one of the twenty republics. They recognize, of course, that individual differences exist among the republics, but do not think these important enough to warrant the preservation of the present political boundaries. They see Latin America as having within it various zones which are geographic regions. Mexico and Central America comprise one such zone. Venezuela, Colombia,

[92] Haya de la Torre, *La defensa continental*, p. 20.
[93] Haya de la Torre, *El antimperialismo y el Apra*, p. 20.
[94] *Ibid.*, p. 176; Haya de la Torre, *¿A dónde va Indoamérica?*, p. 240.
[95] *El pueblo-continente*, p. 76.
[96] *Ibid.*, pp. 75–78.
[97] Haya de la Torre, *Y después de la guerra ¿qué?*, p. 13.

Ecuador, Peru, and Bolivia make up another. Chile, Argentina, Paraguay, and Uruguay compose a third. Brazil would be a fourth. Each of these regions would require special treatment, but the four zones combine to make up a unit having problems which are basically similar; all are producers of either agricultural or mineral raw materials.[98]

The most important Aprista argument for the unification of Latin America is that it would strengthen the area, politically and economically, hence benefit each of the twenty republics. Haya de la Torre points out that the weak North American colonies united and grew into the greatest power in the contemporary world. He writes that at the same time the North American colonies grew strong united, the Latin American colonies remained disunited and weak. His conclusion is that the present weakness of Latin America is a direct result of this disunity and that unification would immediately strengthen the area.[99] He also claims that the rest of the world looks upon Latin America as a unit, treats it as such, and makes its plans for the area upon this basis. Haya, therefore, thinks it is time the Latin Americans began to develop a continental consciousness which would enable them to look upon their area as a unit.[100]

The Apristas contend that unification of Latin America would raise the standard of living of its people by fostering the rapid industrial development of the area. They often say that the Latin Americans are "the poorest people in the world living in the richest part of the world."[101] They maintain that this poverty is a direct result of the way the economy of the area is organized. As they see it, the twenty republics are producers of agricultural and mineral raw materials and importers of manufactured goods. Each of the twenty republics concentrates on the production of one or two commodities, and in many countries it is necessary to import many items that could be grown or produced within that country. In an economic system of this type, the country which produces raw materials sells them on the world market at prices it cannot control, which are usually low, and then buys manufactured articles, sometimes made of its own raw material, at high prices it cannot control. The process usually results in a very low standard of living for the people of a country with this kind of economic organization.[102]

The solution of this problem lies, according to the Apristas, in the economic unification of Latin America. They maintain that an economy

[98] Haya de la Torre, *El antimperialismo y el Apra,* pp. 175–183.
[99] Haya de la Torre, *Y después de la guerra ¿qué?,* p. 7.
[100] *Ibid.,* pp. 13–15.
[101] Luis F. de Las Casas, *Unidad económica indoamericana* (1946), p. 6.
[102] *Ibid.,* pp. 50–54.

should be planned and that regional specialization and intensive production are the true bases of a planned economy. They think it is foolish for a Latin American country to import articles which can be produced within the country. Rather, the Apristas contend, a country generally should import only those articles it cannot produce or cannot produce cheaply and should export only when it needs to import.[103]

The Apristas emphasize that unification of Latin America would create an area large enough to provide a mass market for the products of industry. It would be an area rich in natural resources with much room for a growing population, having a range of climate which would permit growing almost everything needed by the area. Rapid industrialization could be hastened by setting up free trade among the twenty republics and surrounding them with a protective tariff wall.[104]

Recognizing that complete economic union based on a division of production among the various countries cannot be forged overnight, the Apristas suggest steps to approach that goal. They propose the creation of a customs union and a single monetary unit for all of Latin America to be followed by plans for the coördination of the economy.[105] A customs union would help to prepare people for political unification, but even this, the Apristas state, is probably too ambitious a goal to begin with. The weaknesses of the means of communication and the pattern of present trade will prevent any extensive exchange of goods between Argentina and Ecuador, or between Peru and Brazil. The way to begin working together, the Apristas affirm, is for the neighboring countries to make arrangements with one another. These would be slowly extended with the goal being the customs union of all twenty republics. A typical regional group could be formed by Peru, Chile, Ecuador, and Bolivia. These four would try to supply one another with as many commodities as possible. Other regional groupings could be set up.[106]

The second compelling reason for the unification of Latin America, according to the Apristas, is the need for its defense. In a world of economic imperialism, fascist dictators, and communist expansion, the small, weak country is doomed to eventual absorption. The solution which would strengthen Latin America's defenses is union.[107] The writings of the Apristas are not too clear on how union would strengthen Latin America militarily, but as Haya puts it: "Liberty without force is difficult to preserve . . . and force without union is unconceivable."[108]

[103] Saco, *op. cit.*, pp. 135–137.
[104] *Ibid.*, p. 135.
[105] Haya de la Torre, *Y después de la guerra ¿qué?*, pp. 203–204.
[106] Saco, *op. cit.*, pp. 137–138.
[107] Haya de la Torre, *La defensa continental*, p. 33.
[108] *Ibid.*, p. 38.

The Apristas use unification as an argument for strengthening Latin America in the face of all of its difficulties. During the period when United States imperialism was the great threat—according to the Apristas—unification was the solution. Unification would defend Latin America from Nazi aggression. When the war ended and the threat of Russian Communist aggression arose, the Apristas again pointed to unification as the solution.[109]

Another reason unification would benefit Latin America, according to the Apristas, is that it would prevent the possibility of any future armed conflict among the twenty republics.[110] Manuel Seoane claims that there is always a possibility of Latin America becoming the Balkans of the New World if the small states are not combined into one large state.[111]

To the argument that unification would be difficult the Apristas answer that the opposite is true. Haya de la Torre points out that there is no real language barrier except for Brazil and Haiti. He claims there are no really important natural frontiers separating the various republics except in the case of the Caribbean islands.[112] Actually, Haya maintains, unification would be comparatively easy for Latin America if its leaders would only work for it. Latin America, he contends, is not faced with as many difficulties as Italy had to overcome when it united after centuries of war between the Italian states. The United States was able to unite after a bloody civil war. Switzerland, Germany, Britain, and other areas united. Latin America could do likewise, Haya believes.[113]

History properly understood would teach the Latin Americans to unite, the Apristas say. They point to the unity achieved in the struggle for freedom from Spain and ask the question: If we could all battle together under San Martín, Bolívar, and Sucre, why can we not unite now?[114] Unity is as important and essential for Latin America to win its economic independence from imperialism as it was from 1810 to 1824.[115] The lessons of history demonstrate to the Apristas that the world is moving toward ever larger units. They see an evolutionary process from feudal dispersion to the formation of large nation-states, to the demarcation of powerful continental units. Today, the Apristas

---

[109] *La Opinión* (Los Angeles), April 4, 1948, pp. 1, 7.

[110] Haya de la Torre, *Y después de la guerra ¿qué?*, pp. 77–78.

[111] In Luis F. de Las Casas, *op. cit.*, p. 7.

[112] Haya de la Torre, *El antimperialismo y el Apra*, p. 175.

[113] Haya de la Torre, *Política Aprista*, p. 97.

[114] Haya de la Torre, *El antimperialismo y el Apra*, p. 37; El Buró de Redactores de "Cuaderno Aprista," *40 preguntas y 40 respuestas sobre el Partido Aprista Peruano*, p. 12.

[115] Seoane, *Nuestros fines*, p. 30.

affirm, the powerful state is very large, a United States of America, or a Union of Soviet Socialist Republics. They warn that the Latin Americans must learn this lesson taught by history. Since the trend is toward ever larger units only two alternatives exist: the Latin American republics must unite to become strong, or remain disunited and the prey of large, powerful nations.[116]

The Apristas recognize that unification in itself would not solve all of Latin America's problems. They advocate unification because they think it would lay the basis for a higher standard of living for the masses and would strengthen the area. If unification comes voluntarily it would be good, but it could also come when an outside power unites the various countries against their will by conquest.[117]

The Apristas claim two forces work against the unification of the Latin American republics. These are United States imperialism and the ruling oligarchies of the majority of the twenty republics. The Apristas assert that these two culprits are equally guilty and that they coöperate with one another by stirring up conflicts among the various republics.[118] They do not lay the blame for disunity upon the people of either the United States or of Latin America, but rather look to them to help achieve unity.[119]

Haya de la Torre writes that patriotism as a slogan is the stock in trade of every *cacique,* every tyrant, and every oligarchy. The patriotism of such people, Haya claims, is based on hostility to the neighbor and xenophobia. He recalls how he was taught to hate Chile when he was a boy, and how the false patriots in Peru kept talking about the war with Chile long after the event was over. This is not patriotism, says Haya, but it will continue as long as people continue divided as they are.[120]

The Apristas think one obstacle to the unification of Latin America can be described as mental colonialism. They believe that this makes many of the people of the twenty republics ignore their own continent and turn their attention toward Europe and the United States. As a result, the Apristas claim, the young Latin American may know where Dieppe is and not know where Quezaltenango is. He may know about the ruins of Egypt and Pompeii, but not about the ruins of Chichén-

[116] Haya de la Torre, *La defensa continental,* p. 20; Luis F. de Las Casas, *op. cit.,* p. 6.

[117] Haya de la Torre, *¿A dónde va Indoamérica?,* pp. 239–243.

[118] See, for example, "Guatemala y Honduras en conflicto," *Indoamérica,* vol. 1 (August, 1928), 2.

[119] Haya de la Torre, *El antimperialismo y el Apra,* p. 37; Haya de la Torre, *Y después de la guerra ¿qué?,* pp. 85–87.

[120] Haya de la Torre, *Por la emancipación de América Latina,* pp. 111–113.

Itzá, Machu-Picchu, or Chan-Chan. The reason for this, according to the Apristas, is that Latin American schools teach little about the history of Latin America as a whole. The systematic exchange of students among the various republics is not fostered. The press considers information about Latin America unimportant. Latin Americans are accustomed to looking at their countries as islands. The traveler and the student almost always go to Europe or the United States. They seldom think of visiting the other American republics. The Apristas would change this situation by having the press follow a systematic policy of printing information about the other republics. They believe that the children should be taught the history of the twenty republics in a serious manner. The political parties should learn to coöperate. Then union would become an attainable objective.[121]

Despite the fact that their advocacy of unification has failed to produce results, the Apristas remain convinced that this is a necessary step for Latin America. They have suggested, therefore, various measures at different times which would stimulate coöperation among the twenty republics. These measures, in addition to the previously mentioned customs union and single monetary unit, include: a continental bank system;[122] the organization of a unified military force of volunteers from all parts of Latin America to fight against the totalitarian powers;[123] and the creation of a Latin American continental citizenship.[124]

The Apristas repeat the idea of continental unification in all their activities within and without Peru.[125] They think even if they were in power in Peru they could not successfully oppose imperialism without the aid of the other Latin American republics.[126] Their advocacy of this policy of continental unification was the pretext used by successive dictatorships in Peru to deprive the Aprista movement of its liberty of action. It is an international movement, said the dictatorships, and, therefore, cannot be permitted to gain power in Peru. The Aprista

[121] Haya de la Torre, *La defensa continental,* pp. 25–29; Haya de la Torre, *¿A dónde va Indoamérica?*, pp. 144–145.

[122] Haya de la Torre, *La defensa continental,* pp. 179–180.

[123] Haya de la Torre, *Y después de la guerra ¿qué?*, pp. 25–26.

[124] Haya de la Torre, *Política Aprista,* p. 12.

[125] One of the most recent statements made by a leader of the Aprista movement reads as follows: "We have facing us, as so many times, two formidable foreign enemies; two implacable imperialisms: that of Wall Street and that of Moscow; we know that for this struggle we have to unite all the democrats from Alaska to Tierra del Fuego, for the common interest of attaining or preserving liberty, for well-being and justice for our masses exploited until now." Luis Alberto Sánchez, in Conferencia Interamericana pro Democracia y Libertad, *Resoluciones y otros documentos* (1950), p. 117.

[126] Seoane, *Páginas polémicas,* pp. 91–92.

leaders point out that they are accused by non-Peruvian conservatives of trying to Peruvianize the rest of Latin America, while at the same time they are accused by the Peruvian dictatorships of trying to internationalize Peru. Both of these claims are nonsense, according to the Apristas.[127]

After union, the Apristas state, Latin America would become a populous nation living in an immensely rich area. The people would feel united by a common tradition and history. The United States of Latin America would then take its rightful place in world affairs.[128]

THE APRISTA OPINION OF THE PAN AMERICAN UNION

The Apristas favor the unification of Latin America, but they do not support the Pan American Union.[129] They look upon it as an expression of the foreign policy of the United States which spends its time passing innocuous resolutions. Haya de la Torre once called the Pan American Union "a form of imperialism with ornament."[130] On another occasion, he wrote that the Pan American Union was "obsolete and grown old."[131] The two most important weaknesses in the Pan American Union, according to the Aprista leaders, are that it is dominated by the United States and that it is made up of the representatives of governments, many of which are dictatorships.

Haya de la Torre claims that Pan Americanism in practice is the policy of "dollar diplomacy" with the United States businessmen guiding the Secretary of State in his relations with the people of Indoamerica. Since the policy of the "good neighbor" is supposed to have replaced "dollar diplomacy," Haya claims that "Pan Americanism, as it was directed and interpreted since the foundation of the Pan American Union, now has no reason for being."[132] Haya writes, "Pan Americanism is a name which suggests and is associated with the idea of Pan Germanism or 'big-stick!' or as Manuel Ugarte called it, 'Minister of Colonies.' "[133] As can be seen from these comments, Pan Americanism does not signify equality to the Apristas, but rather suggests the confused mixture of past inter-American relations. The Aprista leaders propose, therefore, that the old terminology and organizations be aban-

[127] Partido Aprista Peruano, *op cit.*, pp. xlvi–xlvii; Haya de la Torre, *Política Aprista*, p. 95.

[128] Haya de la Torre, *La defensa continental*, p. 40.

[129] The author has been unable to find an expression of the Aprista opinion of the new Organization of American States.

[130] Haya de la Torre, *Y después de la guerra ¿qué?*, p. 86.

[131] Haya de la Torre, *La defensa continental*, p. 32.

[132] *Ibid.*, pp. 91–92.

[133] *Ibid.*, p. 92.

doned in order to put relations between the United States and Latin America on a basis of equality.

The fact that the Pan American Union permits the representatives of undemocratic governments to sit at the same table as the representatives of democratic governments demonstrates its futility to the Apristas. They claim that the only government which has the right to speak for its people is a democratic government. Therefore, the Pan American conferences display only "diplomatic solidarity."[134] The Apristas seek the solidarity of peoples speaking through their freely elected representatives.

The Aprista opposition to the Pan American Union was strengthened when the American states met in Lima in 1938. Peru at that time was living under a *Ley de Emergencia* and the Apristas were underground, in jail, or in exile. The Apristas claimed that the fact that the Peruvian dictatorship could act as host to a meeting of the Pan American Union demonstrated that that organization was not an expression of the people of America. One of the Aprista publications suggested that the delegates to the Lima conference tour the city and inspect the jails where Apristas were illegally held, the torture cells in the jails, the padlocked Aprista periodicals, and the libraries where the delegates could read the *Ley de Emergencia,* the *Ley de Securidad Interior,* and the *Constitución del Estado.*[135] Haya de la Torre addressed an open letter to the Lima conference asking it to do something about the terror in Peru, but no action was taken. In his letter Haya said, "The Conference of Lima will be a decisive proof. Either Pan Americanism will be transformed from its present base, converting itself into a vast and noble continental doctrine incompatible with imperialism and tyrannies—or it will continue offering the world, in each of its diplomatic assemblies, a new and merry comedy with grandiloquent well-fed actors."[136]

The Apristas repeated this complaint every time the American states met. Haya de la Torre said of the Rio Conference of 1942: "Like all other Pan American conferences, it gave undue weight to the voices of Latin American governments and forgot that on this continent what a government says is not always in accord with what its people think."[137] Luis Enríquez made the same criticism of the Conference of Chapultepec. He pointed out that the representatives of the dictators voted for

[134] Víctor Raúl Haya de la Torre, "Toward a Real Inter-Americanism," *Free World,* III (July, 1942), 164.

[135] *Trinchera Aprista,* vol. 2 (Nov., 1938), 12.

[136] Víctor Raúl Haya de la Torre, *La VIII Conferencia Panamericana ¿Otra comedia? Frente norte indoamericano contra la internacional negra fascista* (1938), pp. 11–12.

[137] Haya de la Torre, "Toward a Real Inter-Americanism," *Free World,* III (July, 1942), 163.

resolutions which, if only a small part of them were put into practice, would bring democracy to America. Enríquez concluded that the Conference of Chapultepec would have to be followed by another conference which would bring free men together to establish a democratic inter-American organization.[138] Haya de la Torre concurred with Enríquez' criticism of the Conference of Chapultepec. He stated that two kinds of resolutions were adopted at the conference. One group of resolutions, he said, "represents the old Pan American diplomacy, while the other is an inter-American attempt to make the countries of America keep pace with others more advanced in democratic ideology. The first set of resolutions is like an anchor trying to hold back the second set, and is likely to give us many a headache in the future."[139]

Haya stated that he thought that "the Pan American Union will have to go, since it survives as an old-fashioned, idealistic, and intellectual organism, of no practical and positive utility. We need in America a dynamic organization able to enforce democratic precepts."[140]

The Apristas present another argument against the concept of the Pan American Union. They say two separate problems are involved in coöperation between the United States and Latin America. One is the problem of the unification of Latin America, everything from the Rio Grande to the tip of the southern continent, including Puerto Rico. This is the problem of continental union or Indoamerica. The other problem is that of the coördination or alliance of the United States of America with the Indoamerican territory not yet united. "The Apristas are not Pan Americanists, but Indoamericanists as regards the continent and inter-Americanists as regards the hemisphere."[141] Haya de la Torre calls the Aprista goal in this respect "an inter-American Democratic Front."[142] Manuel Seoane calls it "democratic inter-Americanism without imperialism."[143]

The Apristas believe that only after the unification of Indoamerica would the United States and Indoamerica be able to coöperate as equals. The one would continue to be a raw-material-producing area, the other a highly industrialized nation. The two would exchange their products and coöperate in defending America from aggressors. Both would benefit from such coöperation, but the union of Indoamerica is an imperative first step in order to make harmonious relations possible.

[138] "A Latin Looks at Chapultepec," *Inter American*, IV (April, 1945), 16–17.
[139] Quoted in *Peruvian Times*, July 6, 1945, p. 2.
[140] *Loc. cit.*
[141] Haya de la Torre, *Y después de la guerra ¿qué?*, p. 86.
[142] Víctor Raúl Haya de la Torre, "An Inter-American Democratic Front," *Free World*, IV (Nov., 1942), 150–152.
[143] Manuel Seoane, "Where Do We Go From Here?," *Inter-American*, V (March, 1946), 25.

FOR THE NATIONALIZATION OF LAND AND INDUSTRY

Opposition to imperialism by a united Latin America is followed in the maximum program advocated by the Apristas by a call for the nationalization of land and industry. This is necessary, they maintain, both as a means of fighting imperialism and as a means toward a just organization of society. In this plank of their platform the Apristas accept the socialist conception as their ideal. Nationalization,[144] as they understand the term, would be some type of state ownership of the wealth-producing factors within society and would create a "Latin America for the Latin Americans."[145] The Apristas see foreign capital owning more and more of the Latin American sources of wealth as the years pass and, therefore, they say that "for the people of Indoamerica it is a question of life and death to acquire the full possession of their wealth."[146] The Apristas writings are not too clear on how nationalization would be carried out, but they are clear that they would like to see this done.[147]

The Apristas do not favor turning foreign property over to native capital after it is nationalized. They favor a form of state ownership which would foster a social system containing more equality and justice than does the capitalist system of the United States and Western Europe. Nationalization is a long-range goal for the Apristas. The important thing to do, they say, is to unite Latin America for the struggle against imperialism. The organization of the economy of Latin America can be decided after union has been accomplished. Each of the twenty republics would create its own minimum program which would contain solutions of all economic problems within the area.[148]

THE INTER-AMERICANIZATION OF THE PANAMA CANAL

The fourth goal of the Aprista maximum program proposes the joint ownership and control of the Panama Canal by all the nations of America.[149] Inter-Americanization of the canal, say the Apristas, would

[144] The Apristas' views on nationalization will be discussed in detail in the next chapter dealing with their program for Peru.

[145] Víctor Raúl Haya de la Torre, *Teoría y táctica del aprismo* (1931), p. 74.

[146] Cossio del Pomar, *op. cit.*, p. 117.

[147] The Apristas applauded the action of the Mexican government in nationalizing the oil industry. At the time this took place, the Argentina Apristas addressed a letter to the Argentine legislature asking it to follow the Mexican example and nationalize the Argentine oil industry. *Trinchera Aprista*, vol. 2 (Nov., 1938), 12.

[148] Cossio del Pomar, *op. cit.*, pp. 116–117; Haya de la Torre, *El antimperialismo y el Apra*, p. 90; Saco, *op. cit.*, pp. 85–100.

[149] The Apristas often use the slogan "For the inter-nationalization of the Panama Canal," but the author has been unable to discover that the Aprista leaders ever advocated world control of the canal. Haya de la Torre writes that "the inter-

aid the Latin American struggle against imperialism and would also help to unite the twenty disunited republics.[150]

The Apristas believe that United States ownership and control of the canal give it control over a large part of the commerce and communications of the Latin American republics. If the canal were put under inter-American control, a great danger to the free economic life of Latin America would be removed. To the objection that the United States does not discriminate against Latin America users of the canal, Haya de la Torre points out that there can always be a change in the policy of the United States. He states that imperialism is fundamentally an economic phenomenon and that it is the elementary duty of Latin America to use all precautions to assure its own independence. He agrees that there is a Good Neighbor Policy, but points out that it is up to the Latin American nations to make sure that the Good Neighbor Policy does not change, "remembering that it is not unlikely that the new [Franklin] Roosevelt policy may become the old [Theodore] Roosevelt policy."[151] If the canal were controlled by all of America, the Apristas maintain, it could never be used by the United States to discriminate against one or all of the Latin American republics if United States policy changes in the future.

Inter-American control of the canal would also strengthen its defenses. In the defense of the canal, the United States seeks the material and moral aid of all of Latin America. Is it not logical to suppose, asks Haya de la Torre, that if the Latin American states share control of the canal they would always be ready to defend it? An attack by a European power upon a canal owned and controlled by all of America would mean an attack upon all of America. If the canal were owned by all America, therefore, there would be no neutrals in the Western Hemisphere if the canal were attacked. Haya de la Torre points out that the German Nazis used the canal in their propaganda in Latin America, promising it to the Latin American states for aiding Germany. Even if such promises are demagogy certain states in Latin America might succumb to this bait and remain neutral rather than defend something they do not consider their property.[152]

---

nationalization of the Panama Canal assumes—according to the Apristas—inter-Americanization, since Aprismo is an exclusively American political doctrine. That is to say, it means the participation of all the states of North America and Indoamerica in the ownership and control of the Canal." *La defensa continental*, pp. 154–155.

[150] Haya de la Torre, "¿Debe internacionalizarse el Canal de Panamá?," *La defensa continental*, pp. 149–164; Haya de la Torre, *El antimperialismo y el Apra*, p. 90; Haya de la Torre, *Y después de la guerra ¿qué?*, p. 203; Cossio del Pomar, *op. cit.*, pp. 117–119.

[151] Haya de la Torre, *La defensa continental*, p. 157.

[152] *Loc. cit.*

Inter-American control of the canal would also aid the general unity of Latin America. "Panama should be the center of the great Bolivarian project of a united America. The ideal of the Liberator will be achieved with the inter-Americanization of the Canal, for in this important geographic bond of the New World will be found a base for a just equilibrium between the United States of the North and the disunited States of the South."[153]

If and when a canal is built in Nicaragua, this, too, should be controlled by all the American states.[154] Control of the Panama Canal and of a Nicaraguan canal, if it is ever constructed, could be lodged in an international company similar to the one that administers the Suez Canal. Each of the American republics would be represented upon this board and each would enjoy the benefits and responsibilities that went with ownership of the canal. If this plan were followed, the Apristas claim, the only thing the United States would lose upon taking the other American republics into partnership would be a few million dollars, which is not important compared to the benefits the United States would receive.[155] The Apristas can see no harmful effects from inter-Americanization of the canal and, they believe, therefore, that the United States should see that this is done as "a concrete demonstration of confidence and sincerity and perpetual 'good-neighborship.' "[156]

FOR SOLIDARITY WITH ALL PEOPLES AND ALL OPPRESSED CLASSES

The Apristas end their maximum program with a call for solidarity with the rest of the world. They feel a kinship between themselves and the colonial peoples, and the working classes of the "capitalist countries." This plank in their platform is no more than a gesture, but they want to tell the world that they are a radical organization which struggles for a better world as other movements and other peoples are doing all over the world.[157]

NONVIOLENCE IN POLITICS

When the Apristas talk of turning their attention to Latin America they do not mean that they intend to imitate the previous course of Latin American politics, for that has been an alternation of anarchy, violence, and dictatorship. What they want is to stimulate Peruvians

[153] *Ibid.*, p. 163.
[154] Haya de la Torre, *El antimperialismo y el Apra*, pp. 90–91.
[155] Haya de la Torre, *La defensa continental*, p. 160.
[156] *Ibid.*, p. 156.
[157] Cossio del Pomar, *op. cit.*, p. 119; Haya de la Torre, *El antimperialismo y el Apra*, pp. 91–94.

and other Latin Americans into serious thinking which can spark an interest in democratic government. They want the Aprista movement to be a "party of ideas,"[158] and hope that it can stimulate an educational renovation which will foster constitutional government in Peru and the rest of Latin America. They insist, therefore, that the attainment of power must be a peaceful process. They recognize that Peru and the other Latin American republics have had too many civil wars, too many caudillos, and too much undemocratic government. They often say, "We do not want to acquire power by violence."[159] Does this mean the Apristas are pacifists and are opposed to the use of all violence in politics?

In Trujillo, in 1932, the Apristas defended themselves by military means so successfully that it required the combined efforts of the army and air force to overcome their resistance. Many times Haya de la Torre and other leaders of the organization shot their way out of police traps during the years they lived in hiding.[160] Various dictatorships in Peru have accused the Apristas of participating in many armed revolts and of being murderers and gangsters.[161] Despite these charges, which have never been proved, the writings of the Apristas are clear upon this issue. They advocate coming to power by peaceful means, preferably by means of an election.

The leadership of the Aprista movement believes that the means it uses help to determine the end achieved and, therefore, it is opposed to the idea that the end justifies the means.[162] Because it wants to educate the people of Peru it tries to use educational methods to get its ideas across. The Apristas ask their opponents to debate the issues in order to clarify them. They state they want their movement to be one that has succeeded "in finding more worthy and more sane methods of struggle" than are customarily used in Peruvian politics.[163] They desire to use as their force the enthusiasm of the people. They wish their organization to leave an example for the future, an example that it is possible to respect the law yet make an impression upon the people.[164]

The Apristas disclaim violence and at the same time they insist their movement is revolutionary. They maintain that it is "possible to be revolutionary and to make a revolution without resorting to violence."[165] Haya de la Torre often points to Christ, Tolstoy, and Gandhi as ex-

[158] Seoane, *Páginas polémicas,* pp. 18–19.
[159] Víctor Raúl Haya de la Torre, quoted in the New York *Times,* July 12, 1931, p. 1.
[160] Cossio del Pomar, *op. cit.,* pp. 328, 351–353.
[161] *Supra,* p. 19, n. 60.
[162] Partido Aprista Peruano, *op. cit.,* p. 51.
[163] Haya de la Torre, *Política Aprista,* p. 71.
[164] *Ibid.,* p. 74.
[165] *Ibid.,* p. 92.

amples of nonviolent revolutionaries, and he is fond of quoting Engels' remark that it is possible that the revolution in Britain will be peaceful. Haya, of course, recognizes that violence can attend a revolutionary change, but he and the other leaders of the movement insist that they oppose violence for its own sake and are opposed to a revolution just to obtain power. They claim they desire power in order to make a revolutionary change in the organization of Peruvian society.[166]

When the dictatorship headed by General Maximiliano Hernández Martínez in El Salvador was overthrown by a civil disobedience movement which developed into a general strike, Haya de la Torre published an article[167] in which he applauded this method of fighting dictatorship. As he saw the Salvadorean movement, it was "the best means for hastening wholesome and educational changes toward liberty which avoided great bloodshed."[168] The general strike and civil disobedience were based on the kind of moral force the Apristas were trying to stimulate and, he believed, should become a regular part of the means used to win liberty in Latin America.[169]

The author asked Haya de la Torre why the Apristas never attempted to take power through an armed revolution. His reply was that although the Apristas were not pacifists, they were convinced that the experience of history demonstrated that the use of violence in politics exposed its users to the danger of degenerating into complete dependence upon violence. Haya said the experience of the Russian revolution was of great importance in this respect. There, according to Haya, force was used to get and to keep power for the Bolsheviks. As a result, all the noble aims of the Russian revolution have been forgotten and power is the important consideration in all the activity of the Russian government. He went on to say that this seemed to demonstrate that the means used to achieve an end were so important in determining the end achieved that the Apristas refused to take any chance of degenerating by becoming a violent organization. Haya stated that the Apristas had no interest in getting rid of the Peruvian dictatorship in order to set up another dictatorship even if they would be the dictators.[170]

Haya has repeated this idea many times in his writings. After the 1931 election, many of the Apristas, enraged at being cheated out of

---

[166] *Ibid.*, pp. 92–93. See also Haya de la Torre, "La no violencia de Gandhi como método de hacer la guerra," *Ex-combatientes y desocupados*, pp. 139–143.

[167] "La huelga general como arma de la revolución democrática," reprinted in *Y después de la guerra ¿qué?*, pp. 150–158.

[168] *Ibid.*, p. 157.

[169] *Ibid.*, pp. 150–158.

[170] Personal interview with Víctor Raúl Haya de la Torre, Los Angeles, California, April 1, 1948.

victory, wanted to use arms to prevent Sánchez Cerro from taking office. This was not done because the leaders of the Aprista movement did not think force would benefit the movement.[171] Haya pointed out at the time that the Aprista movement was not created to elect him president.[172] He claims that despite all the violence used against the Aprista movement, it has used only legal means to protest such violence. The Apristas want to debate their opponents—and they demand democracy—because they have confidence that their ideas would win out.[173]

SYMBOLISM

In line with their preoccupation with the reality of Latin America, the Apristas strive to embody their philosophy in simple symbols that even the most illiterate Indian can understand. They have done this consciously from the day in 1924 when Haya first proposed the creation of the Alianza Popular Revolucionaria Americana. They have their own flag, salute, and songs.

The symbolism began with the Aprista flag. Since the ultimate goal is to unite all of Latin America, the flag consists of a reproduction of Indoamerica (everything from the Rio Grande to the southern tip of the continent) in gold, surrounded by a gold ring upon a background of red.[174] The outline of the Indoamerican continent, surrounded by a ring, is also used as a symbol to decorate Aprista pamphlets and periodicals.[175]

The Apristas have a group of these symbols. One that they often use is a stylized condor with four wings on either side, sometimes containing a five-pointed star in the center on which are the letters APRA.

[171] Cossio del Pomar, *op. cit.*, pp. 251–252.

[172] In Sánchez, *Raúl Haya de la Torre o el político*, p. 198.

[173] Felipe Cossio del Pomar, *Datos biográficos de Haya de la Torre* (1946), pp. 43, 47. Hubert Herring, after close study of Peru, asked the question, "Why does not Apra, with the majority of coherent Peruvians behind it, rise in its power and take over the government?" His answer was that a good army and certain forces in Peru support the government. "The second reason," he wrote, "is found in the character of the movement and the leader: Haya has no taste for bloodletting; he believes in peace, believes that the just cause will triumph, believes in the virtue of patience. His critics, knowing the strength of his following, put him down as a fool, never as a weakling. Many of his friends aver that he has permitted opportunity to pass by, that he should have seized power before Benavides built up his army and police." *Good Neighbors*, p. 268.

[174] A picture in color of the flag appears on the cover of Haya de la Torre, *La defensa continental.* A picture of the ceremony of Haya presenting the original flag to Mexican students on May 7, 1924, appears in Cossio del Pomar, *Datos biográficos de Haya de la Torre*, p. 32. See also Sánchez, *Raúl Haya de la Torre o el político*, p. 110; Cossio del Pomar, *Haya de la Torre, el indoamericano*, p. 111.

[175] Haya de la Torre, *El antimperialismo y el Apra*, cover; José H. Cháves S., *Voces de la ruta heroica* (1947), cover; it appears on the masthead of *Trinchera Aprista* and *Apra*, two Aprista periodicals.

The condor has embossed on it geometric designs patterned after Indian motifs.[176] The condor also is worn as a lapel pin and identifying badge.[177] Sometimes a red five-pointed star is used as a symbol either alone or with the letters APRA arranged to form a circle within the star.[178]

The Apristas use a salute which consists of bringing the left arm up over the head, palm of the hand open, facing forward.[179] They end most of their speeches and letters with the slogan "Only Aprismo Will Save Peru" (*Sólo el aprismo salvará al Perú*) which is sometimes abbreviated as SEASAP.[180] They have worked this slogan into one of their songs, "Pueblo Peruano."[181]

The most popular Aprista slogan is the word Apra. Carleton Beals reports that he saw it carved on the high cliffs of the Andes, painted on roofs, spelled out in sand plants on desert roads, even branded on a dog.[182] Blair Niles reports that she saw Apra painted in large, red letters on the walls of the fortress of Sacsahuamán.[183] James Ullman reports that he saw Apra painted on the concrete base of an abandoned wireless station on the summit of San Cristóbal.[184]

Haya de la Torre, the jefe of the Aprista movement, is utilized in the Aprista symbolism. Christopher Morley reports seeing little pottery busts of Haya de la Torre on sale in the Lima market.[185] Haya's picture is on display at the Aprista meetings. His birthday, February 22, is made into a holiday and is utilized to popularize the movement with special meetings and special issues of the Aprista publications.[186]

The Apristas have a series of songs, designed both to instruct and enthuse, which are sung at their meetings and rallies. Among these

---

[176] Cháves S., *op. cit.*, back cover; Julio Garrido Malaver, *Canto a la navidad* (1945), p. 31.

[177] The author examined those worn by Haya de la Torre and Alfredo Saco in personal interviews: with Haya on April 1, 1948; with Saco on February 1, 1948.

[178] Carlos Manuel Cox (editor), *Cartas de Haya de la Torre a los prisioneros Apristas* (1946), front cover; Fernando León de Vivero, *Avance del imperialismo fascista en el Perú* (1938), back cover.

[179] Picture of Haya and others saluting in Cossio del Pomar, *Datos biográficos de Haya de la Torre,* p. 54; Manuel Seoane, "Return of an Exile," *Inter-American,* I (Oct., 1942), 44.

[180] Examples in Cox (ed.), *op. cit.*, pp. 71, 79, 95; Professor Inman reports that the Cuban Apristas used the slogan, "Only Aprismo will save Cuba," Samuel Guy Inman, *Latin America, Its Place in World Life* (1937), p. 279. A picture showing this phrase "SEASAP" painted on a wall is seen in *Los crímenes del Sancho-Civilismo, la revolución de Huaraz* (1933), p. 43.

[181] *Cancionero Aprista*, p. 8; see also back cover (n.d.).

[182] Carleton Beals, *Fire on the Andes* (1934), p. 191.

[183] Blair Niles, *Peruvian Pageant* (1937), p. 175.

[184] James R. Ullman, *The Other Side of the Mountain* (1938), p. 61.

[185] Christopher Morley, *Hasta la vista* (1935), p. 71.

[186] See, for example, *Apra "Faj,"* Feb. 22, 1935; *Trinchera Aprista*, vol. 2 (Feb., 1938); a meeting of the Mexican Apristas celebrating Haya's birthday is reported in *Trinchera Aprista*, vol. 2 (March, 1938), 3.

songs is an Apra march; a song about the Universidades Populares González Prada; a song asking for elections; and several songs lauding the Aprista movement. Their most popular song is the Aprista Marseillaise which was intended to be a song for all of Latin America.[187]

The Apristas believe that America is so different from the rest of the world, and in particular from Europe, that it needs a program based on its own peculiar reality. The program offered by the Apristas to meet this need includes opposition to imperialism, an emphasis upon the need of unifying Latin America, nationalizing the land and industry, and inter-Americanizing the Panama Canal. The Aprista program emphasizes the need for nonviolent political activity and is presented in such a way that the most illiterate and backward Indian is able to understand what the Aprista movement proposes to do.[188] On the basis of these general ideas, the Apristas then worked out a specific program for the reorganization of Peru.

---

[187] *Cancionero Aprista;* see Appendix A, p. 133, for the words to Aprista Marseillaise.

[188] See Appendix B, p. 134, for examples of how the Apristas try to compress their ideas into simple slogans.

CHAPTER IV

A PROGRAM FOR PERU

THE APRISTA minimum program, or program for Peru, is worked out in much greater detail than the maximum program for Latin America. This is natural since the Aprista movement is Peruvian and the enforced abstinence of its leaders from political life for long periods gave them much time during which they developed detailed plans and programs which they hoped to put into effect when the Aprista movement came to power. The Apristas pride themselves on not being a party of dreamers, but rather a party of realistic men who want to accomplish something.[1] The leaders of the movement are proud that they spent their years of exile reading books and studying social problems.[2] They are eager to solve every problem facing the country, and as a result they have suggestions to make about every aspect of Peruvian life from the personal behavior of the individual to international relations.

APRISMO IS MORE THAN A POLITICAL PARTY

As has been pointed out, the Apristas maintain that Peru needs to find a completely new system of governmental and economic organization.[3] They see Peru's great curse as the attempt by its governments to maintain the status quo through the use of ignorance and force. This idea stems from the Apristas' search for the reality of Peru. They view Peru as an area where the imposition of Spanish rule by force created a society based on injustice. The Apristas maintain that the present Peruvian ruling caste cannot comprehend anything but a continuation of this unjust, old way of life.[4] The Apristas stigmatize the old way of life as corrupt, as feudally backward, and as dictatorial. They maintain that power is a business to the Peruvian ruling class and that the crisis in Peru is primarily a moral crisis.[5] Haya de la Torre described Peru, in 1939, as "sick with corruption and betrayal. It is a body full of pus."[6] On another occasion, in 1943, Haya claimed that Peru's way of life was as fascist as life in Germany or Italy. Peru, he wrote, had its dictators,

[1] Manuel Seoane, *Nuestros fines* (1931), p. 22.
[2] *Ibid.*, p. 12.
[3] *Supra*, p. 36.
[4] Manuel Seoane, *Páginas polémicas* (1931), pp. 13–15; Víctor Raúl Haya de la Torre, *Y después de la guerra ¿qué?* (1946), pp. 143–147.
[5] Carlos Manuel Cox (ed.), *Cartas de Haya de la Torre a los prisioneros Apristas* (1946), pp. 33–34; Seoane, *Páginas polémicas*, pp. 5–8; Mario de Bernaschina, "Entrevista con Haya de la Torre," *Revista de América* (1943), p. 79.
[6] In an interview with John T. Whitaker, in *Americas to the South* (1939), p. 28.

its concentration camps, its free circulation of fascist literature, and its fascist police mission from the Italian OVRA.[7] Peru, in short, according to the Apristas, is corrupt and needs to be made over.[8]

As a reaction to the corruption the Apristas see in Peru, they attempt to make their movement into something more than an ordinary political party which seeks power. They try to make their party into a way of life with its distinctive philosophy and morals.[9] The Apristas see themselves as soldiers in a crusade, as seekers of an educational purification which will transform Peru from a corrupt, backward country into a modern, democratic nation which will stimulate a flowering of culture. The Apristas are interested in economics and a high standard of living, but even more important than that, they want to see a spiritual renovation within Peru which will create a new country based on a morally changed people. "The world," they say, "does not wish for bread alone because man does not live by bread alone."[10] What the people of the world are seeking, according to the Apristas, is a way of life that contains both economic and spiritual satisfaction within it. The Apristas, who have slogans for most of their main ideas, say that what the world needs is bread and liberty and, therefore, they try to create a situation in which the Peruvian people will be able to enjoy both of these basic needs.[11]

The Apristas try to make faith the motivating force of their movement; faith that a better world can be created. By better they seem to mean better in the sense that the new Peru will be more just to the ordinary person. Antenor Orrego, one of the Aprista leaders, claims that the creation of this faith is what is important about the Aprista

[7] Haya de la Torre, "En Europa y en el Perú he visto actuar al fascismo," *Y después de la guerra ¿qué?*, pp. 147–150.

[8] Professor Herman G. James says of corruption in Latin America: "The common attitude of the colonial governors was that the colonies were theirs for exploitation and for personal gain. In many cases the royal grants were distinctly on those terms: the crown wanted its share, but apart from this the grantees were in complete control. To despoil the natives and the colonists for personal gain was quite orthodox; to rob the crown of some of its percentage was regarded as dangerous perhaps but not reprehensible. The concept of a government post as an opportunity for personal gain rather than as an obligation of public service inevitably became accepted by the elements that formed the governing class in the days of independence. The widespread existence of political corruption in Latin America, which is very generally admitted and regretted by Latin American writers, is in large part a heritage of this colonial administration." "Government: Latin America," *Encyclopedia of the Social Sciences*, vol. 7 (1932), 89. Quoted with permission of The Macmillan Company.

[9] Fernando León de Vivero, "Perú revolucionario," *Trinchera Aprista*, vol. 2 (Feb., 1938), 5.

[10] Haya de la Torre, *Y después de la guerra ¿qué?*, p. 135; Seoane, "Aprismo significa renovación," *Páginas polémicas*, pp. 12–13.

[11] One of their slogans is "Neither bread without liberty nor liberty without bread." Haya de la Torre, *Y después de la guerra ¿qué?*, p. 137.

movement. He writes that the Aprista movement was able to create faith within a people living without a goal in life. This faith in a better life, he continues, has been able to canalize the spiritual and moral force within the Peruvian people to strive toward that goal.[12] Manuel Seoane, another leader of the Aprista movement, points out that Peru has been so full of skepticism that the faith of the Apristas becomes a great moral force.[13]

Inspired by this faith, the Apristas say that "the Peruvian Aprista Party aspires to national renovation through the progress and well-being of all Peruvians; through the education of the eighty per cent of our people who do not know how to read or write; through the material and spiritual redemption of our people by the improvement of its youth."[14] The ideal of the Aprista movement is "a free, just, enlightened, and great country."[15] The way to accomplish this end, according to the Aprista writings, is for the Aprista movement to become a moral force.[16] They say, "The Peruvian Aprista Party or Party of the People is a national force vigorously organized and educationally disciplined. *It is a school of life* [italics mine], a way of conduct, and of civic action. It is not a partisan political movement without vital roots. The Aprista must be before all a responsible man of strong moral texture. He must be a man with CLEAN HANDS and with a clear and high consciousness of his patriotic and social duties. He should be pure, he should be valiant, he should be HEROIC."[17] This reasoning is repeated throughout the Aprista writings.[18]

The Apristas say they are not primarily interested in power, but rather in education. Haya de la Torre once described the Aprista goal in this way: "Anyone may arrive at the Palace because the road which leads to it may be bought with gold or it may be conquered with guns. But the mission of Aprismo was to get into the conscience of the people before arriving at the Palace."[19] As a result of this reasoning, the Apristas attempt to create a completely honest movement motivated by the highest ideals. They try to make their party into a brotherhood.[20]

[12] Antenor Orrego, *El pueblo-continente* (1939), pp. 122–125.
[13] In Fergac (ed.), *Aprismo* (1933), p. 91.
[14] El Buró de Redactores de "Cuaderno Aprista," *40 preguntas y 40 respuestas sobre el Partido Aprista Peruano* (1941), p. 4.
[15] *Ibid.*, p. 32.
[16] *Ibid.*, p. 16; Seoane, *Páginas polémicas*, p. 15; Víctor Raúl Haya de la Torre, *Política Aprista* (1933), pp. 68–70.
[17] El Buró de Redactores de "Cuaderno Aprista," *op. cit.*, p. 5.
[18] Felipe Cossio del Pomar, *Haya de la Torre, el indoamericano* (1946), pp. 133, 137; Seoane, *Páginas polémicas*, pp. 15–17; Cox (ed.), *op. cit.*, p. 68.
[19] Haya de la Torre, *Política Aprista*, p. 82.
[20] Seoane, *Páginas polémicas*, p. 9.

Included in the slogans which they popularize are:

One for all, all for one.
The Apristas should be mentally and physically strong.
Brothers in struggle, brothers in sorrow, brothers in victory.[21]

The Apristas advocate clean living for their followers. Haya de la Torre writes, "It is necessary to have a brain like a refrigerator: well nourished and well cooled. For that, the comrades should guard their health, exercise, organize hikes, swim, and so forth, as indispensable Aprista discipline. They should, besides, have great control over themselves, they should not dissipate nor give themselves up to the laxness and licentiousness of the tropics."[22]

The leaders of the Aprista movement teach that to be a good Aprista one must be honorable.[23] One must "read, study, think, discipline the mind more and more and strengthen the spiritual powers."[24] They have a complete list of rules for Apristas to follow which includes such items as: warning members not to use the Aprista name in order to improve their private business; asking the intellectuals not to look down upon the workers; urging members not to associate with conservative Peruvian elements; appealing to them to maintain discipline; and many others.[25]

A good source for this aspect of the Aprista ideology is the list of rules drawn up for the guidance of the members of the Aprista youth organization. Here can be seen the rules of action the Aprista movement endeavors to have its youthful followers make a part of their lives. The rules begin: "Apra youth: Prepare yourself for action and not for pleasure. This is thy law." Then follow forty-eight rules of personal conduct for Aprista youth. These include such precepts as: Tell the truth. Be punctual. Do not use foul language. Love the oppressed people of Peru, America, and the world. Be brave, fair, and daring. Make reading a habit. Criticize yourself and learn to take criticism from others. Conduct yourself so that Aprismo will be seen as a complete renovation of personality. Do not play cards. Avoid sexual licentiousness. Love nature. Wash yourself. Sleep enough. Do not smoke. Do not chew coca. Do not drink alcohol.[26]

---

[21] Cossio del Pomar, *op. cit.*, p. 292; Cox (ed.), *op. cit.*, p. 9.
[22] In Cox (ed.), *op. cit.*, p. 24.
[23] El Buró de Redactores de "Cuaderno Aprista," *op. cit.*, p. 2.
[24] Cox (ed.), *op. cit.*, p. 63.
[25] Rómulo Meneses, *Aprismo femenino peruano* (1934), pp. 49–50; see also *Cartilla Aprista* (n.d.), p. 15.
[26] Partido Aprista Peruano, Federación Aprista Juvenil, *Código de acción FAJ* (1934), pp. 4–8. The complete list is found in Appendix C, pp. 135–137. The same rules are published by the Cuban Apristas for their youth movement. Federación Aprista Juvenil, *Código de vida de la F.A.J.* (1937).

The personal habits and ideals advocated by the Aprista movement help give it its crusading character. The Apristas propose to transform Peru from a nation of oppressed into a nation of free men, and they recognize the fact that they face a difficult task. They advocate, therefore, the individual transformation, the need for the Aprista to study, to think, and to prepare for the new society of the future. They point out that their ideals are high and that no great ideal was ever easily achieved.[27] Haya de la Torre even compared the Apristas, persecuted by the Peruvian dictatorship, to Christ suffering on the Cross. Haya's conclusion was that just as Christ had to suffer to accomplish his aims so the Apristas must suffer to accomplish their aim: the moral regeneration of Peru.[28]

Haya de la Torre advises the Apristas to look upon themselves as the potential leaders of Peru. He states that there are only about 500,000 Apristas and about 7,000,000 Peruvians. If the Apristas educate, train, and prepare themselves to be leaders, they would be able to learn how to win the support of the Peruvian people and then be able to educate and organize them to transform Peru. Haya and the other leaders of the organization point out that the Peruvian people are disorganized by their backwardness, their illiteracy, their poverty, and their hunger. The Peruvian people need leaders, and the Aprista movement tries to create a leadership.[29] Professor Inman gave an example of how the Apristas tried to prepare themselves. He reported—in 1933 when the Aprista movement was permitted to function openly for a short time—"Haya and his 'cabinet members' met regularly to discuss the country's business with the same seriousness which they expected to display when eventually called to rule."[30]

A story is told about Haya de la Torre which illustrates the long-range viewpoint of the Apristas. Once when Haya was addressing a political rally, a woman, holding a baby in her arms, spoke against the Apristas. Haya is reported to have told the woman that she could be opposed to Aprismo, but the child in her arms would grow up to be an Aprista.[31] On another occasion, Haya de la Torre illustrated the messianic character of the movement by saying, "We have a right to be proud of our great Party. In this country of depravity, corruption, and embezzlement of public funds; in this country of crime and shame there has appeared a force pressed forward by the people, which is completely

[27] Cox (ed.), *op. cit.*, pp. 68–69.
[28] In *ibid.*, p. 14.
[29] *Ibid.*, pp. 30–31.
[30] Samuel Guy Inman, *Latin America, Its Place in World Life* (rev. ed., 1942), p. 161.
[31] Luis Alberto Sánchez, *Raúl Haya de la Torre o el político* (1934), p. 190.

pure, completely the spirit of justice, completely the sense of reality. And the nearsighted have failed to understand it."[32]

In line with the attempt to make the Aprista movement into a moral force, the organization tries to win the support of the women of the country. The Aprista party proudly claims that it was the first political organization in Peru to accept women as members, and it has always tried to stimulate the political activity of women.[33] Equality for women is given a prominent position in Aprista propaganda, and the domestic program contains carefully worked out planks relating to women's problems. The Apristas oppose the conservative idea that woman's place is in the home and advocate the full integration of women into the life of the country.

The Apristas, then, propose to transform Peru into a modern democratic state both by modifying the individual Peruvian and by instituting certain political and social reforms. They advocate that every Aprista develop a sound mind in a sound body and become dedicated to the task of working for ends which benefit the group rather than the individual. They often use such phrases as "redeeming our Peru"[34] to describe their goal. This aspect of the Aprista ideology transforms the movement into more than an ordinary political party.

The Domestic Program

To reach their goal the Apristas try to develop a program that is a true reflection of Peruvian conditions. They desire a program that is elastic and relative, since, they say, events are moving too fast to permit one to create a perfect program at one sitting.[35] The Apristas admire and follow the practice of democratic political parties in other countries, which hold conventions before each election in order to formulate a program. The Apristas try to make their program a reflection of the sentiment of the entire organization and of all the worth-while elements in Peru. This is done, according to the Apristas, not only to create a realistic program, but also to break the domination of Lima. A program emanating from all of Peru, they maintain, will more accurately reflect the needs of the country than the programs produced by the conservative parties, which are usually written by a few individuals sitting around a table in a café or in an aristocratic club in Lima.[36]

---

[32] Haya de la Torre, *Política Aprista*, p. 167.
[33] Meneses, *op. cit., passim.*
[34] Seoane, *Nuestros fines*, p. 27.
[35] One of the reasons the Apristas give for opposing the Communists is that the Communists claim to have a perfect program which can be used everywhere—Russia, Peru, China, and all other countries.
[36] Seoane, *Nuestros fines*, pp. 27–29.

The Apristas advocate their maximum program within Peru as the long-range goal toward which the country should strive.[37] They do this because they are convinced the Peruvian people and the people of the other nineteen republics are confronted by the same enemies, the foreign imperialists and their accomplices, the native, feudal-minded dictators. The Peruvian people, the Apristas maintain, must coöperate with all the people of Latin America to achieve a new emancipation. Just as unity was needed from 1810 to 1824 in order to defeat Spain, so unity is needed now.[38]

Within Peru the Apristas stress the ultimate goal of the unification of Latin America. As Haya de la Torre puts it, "The basis of all effective democracy and of all possible social justice in our nations is to be found in their political and economic union. While we live 'Balkanized' we will be the Rumanias and Bulgarias, the Serbias and Albanias of this part of the world."[39] The movement for the unification of Latin America, the Apristas contend, is only an attempt to carry out the ideas of Bolívar, and they claim that they are the true interpreters of the destiny of Latin America.[40] The Apristas make clear the fact that since Peru lives as part of an international economic system which plays a decisive role in politics it "cannot separate itself from the problems of Latin America and Latin America is not able to separate itself from the problems of the world."[41]

Unification of Latin America is the main goal of the Apristas, but within their long-range program they construct their minimum or domestic program for Peru. They propose to transform Peru into a functional democracy which will incorporate the entire population into the economic and political life of the country.[42] A good, short description of the domestic program is given by Manuel Seoane:

> ... basically we aspire to the liberation of our human capital, the worker, ... from the economic slavery that weighs on him. Since the Indian constitutes the majority of the population we must win his economic freedom as a first step.... Our true capital is not only the Peruvian citizen but also the riches of our soil which is also enslaved. The principal Peruvian products, our copper, petroleum, cotton, and sugar, are monopolized by imperialistic enterprises or by creole minorities who exploit and tax the country without giving it any benefit, but rather leaving a sorry trail of arbitrari-

[37] See Declaration of Principles in *Resoluciones de la convención de dirigentes del Partido Aprista Peruano, reunida en Lima, Perú, 1942* (1942), p. 7. This declaration is the five-point maximum program.

[38] Seoane, *Nuestros fines*, p. 30; Haya de la Torre, *Política Aprista*, p. 99; Víctor Raúl Haya de la Torre, *El antimperialismo y el Apra* (1936), p. 191; *supra*, chap. iii.

[39] Haya de la Torre, *Y después de la guerra ¿qué?*, p. 237.

[40] Haya de la Torre, *Política Aprista*, p. 100.

[41] *Ibid.*, p. 36.

[42] *Ibid.*, p. 100.

ness, theft, and abuse. This constructive work cannot be completed within the archaic mold of the present Peruvian institutions nor with the men who by their acts or their refusal to permit others to act have led Peru to ruin. This constructive work must be completed by breaking the selfish centralism of Lima with a system of scientific, administrative decentralization by the young and honorable forces of the country.[43]

The Apristas apparently believe that a modern, democratic government in Peru would be able to liberate the forces which would encourage the full development of the Peruvian economy. They maintain that Peru contains the basic requisites for the development of a modern industrial system—people and raw materials. As Haya de la Torre puts it, Peru has "a population capable of producing and a population capable of consuming."[44] The Apristas propose to arrange matters so that the Peruvians could produce more and consume more. They think this could be done by introducing their domestic program.

The first outline of their domestic program was given in the document adopted at the first national congress of the Partido Aprista Peruano in 1931.[45] Since that time they have amplified this basic program and commented on it in books, pamphlets, and periodicals, but they still look back to this original formulation as the basis of their program for Peru.[46]

THE PROPOSED STATE

The Apristas view the present Peruvian state as a class state, as an instrument used by the dominating class to oppress the majority of the population. They consider their most important task, therefore, the conquest of state power as a first prerequisite in order to achieve their goal of social justice for all Peruvians.[47]

Haya de la Torre has compared the state in Latin America to a railroad which is moving and constructing its road at the same time. He points out that the governments of stable countries, such as Britain or the United States, function no matter which party is in control of the governmental apparatus. In Latin America, he continues, no stable

[43] Seoane, *Nuestros fines*, p. 31.

[44] Víctor Raúl Haya de la Torre, *Construyendo el aprismo* (1933), p. 88.

[45] The Aprista "Plan de acción inmediata o programa mínimo," reprinted in Haya de la Torre, *Política Aprista*, pp. 9–29; hereafter cited as *Plan de acción*. Haya de la Torre said of this document: "Our Party approved its minimum program, or *Plan de Acción Inmediata* at the first National Aprista Congress in 1931, after the holding of twenty Departmental Congresses which collected the points of view and resolutions of the Apristas of all the Provinces of Peru." *¿A dónde va Indoamérica?* (1935), p. 270.

[46] The 1931 plan was being popularized as late as 1948 when it was reprinted in the Aprista almanac for that year. *Almanaque la tribuna 1948*, pp. 218–228.

[47] Haya de la Torre, *El antimperialismo y el Apra*, p. 189; Fergac (ed.), *op. cit.*, pp. 82, 132; Luis Alberto Sánchez, *Carta a una indoamericana, cuestiones elementales del aprismo* (1932), p. 11.

governmental apparatus exists and, therefore, governments must follow an erratic course, using instinct to guide developments. He claims that the holders of power have no program except that of staying in power and, likewise, the revolutions which occur from time to time have no program. The oligarchies in Latin America stay in power, Haya claims, by using force and when they grow weak a new force overthrows the old and the government continues as before.[48]

The Apristas propose to end this situation. They state that they do not seek power to continue the old order with the only change being that Apristas would replace the old holders of power. They propose to transform the state, when in control, so that it would become a functioning part of a living democracy. They visualize the ends of the state as "guaranteeing the life, health, moral and material well-being, education, liberty, and economic emancipation of the working classes; and attempting to abolish the exploitation of man by man in a gradual manner as circumstances will permit."[49]

The history of Peru presents, to the Apristas, a picture of the state controlled by two groups which alternate in control of power: the rich, feudal landowners and the militarists. The Apristas claim that to the landowners all Peruvians are peons, and to the militarists all Peruvians are recruits. The Apristas propose to transform the state so it may become responsive to the democratic wishes of the population.[50] The Aprista program declares that when there is a conflict between the rights of an individual and the needs of the community the needs of the majority must prevail.[51]

The Aprista state would be democratic. It would allow complete freedom for all the people of Peru. No censorship of any kind would occur and complete freedom of the press, of speech, and of meeting would exist.[52] The Aprista state would be based upon a system of democratic political parties which, according to the Apristas, has always been missing from Peru. They believe that this lack has contributed to the failure of democracy in Peru. The Apristas maintain that political parties are an essential need in any democratic state. They are the mechanism the

---

[48] Haya de la Torre, *Construyendo el aprismo,* pp. 137–141.

[49] *Plan de acción,* p. 10.

[50] El Buró de Redactores de "Cuaderno Aprista," *op. cit.*, p. 10; Haya de la Torre, *Política Aprista*, p. 56.

[51] *Plan de acción,* p. 10.

[52] Víctor Raúl Haya de la Torre, describing the Aprista state, in the *Peruvian Times*, July 6, 1945, p. 20. Haya also describes the democratic functioning he desires in his *Message to the Nation* of February 15, 1942, when he called on President Manuel Prado y Ugarteche to institute democracy in Peru. *Message to the Nation* by the Chief of the Peruvian Aprista Party. (Translated and mimeographed by the Office of Inter-American Relations, Stanford University, California.)

people use to make democracy work. That is the reason, according to the Apristas, the ruling cliques all over Latin America have tried to prevent the formation of true political parties. As a classic example, the Apristas point to Mexico's dictator, General Porfirio Díaz, whose regime was supposed to be conducted by individuals who were not interested in politics. In the same way, they say, every dictator talks about the nonpolitical character of his regime. This is nonsense to the Apristas. Politics is an indispensable part of democracy. Differences of opinion always exist. In a democracy the parties canalize the differences; in a dictatorship the differences are smothered. Totalitarian governments set up a single party which they use to control a country. The dictators of Latin America do not even do that but govern by whim.[53]

Democracy, then, is a primary goal for the new state the Apristas wish to create. They disagree with all who argue that Latin America is not ready for democracy. Seoane says, in this respect: "Some people claim that, unlike the Anglo-Saxons, the Latin American people are not ready for democracy. They may be right. But they forget that when the Anglo-Saxons began to practice democracy a century or two ago they were just as backward as we may be now." Then Seoane continues: "Democracy is not a prize that is awarded to the politically mature. It is a training school for the politically adolescent. Democracy is a tool, a means of making steady progress."[54] This statement clearly presents the Aprista opinion of democracy. To them democracy is a mechanism which would permit the Aprista state to learn from its errors and provide the mass support which is essential to progress toward a modern state.

To make democracy effective the Apristas propose the use of the secret ballot in all elections. They favor eighteen as the age for attainment of voting rights. They advocate that women exercise full political rights, including that of holding all elective and appointive governmental positions.[55]

The Apristas use various terms to designate the new state which they propose to create in Peru. Sometimes it is the Aprista state.[56] It has been called the school-state which will teach the population.[57] At times the Apristas call it the anti-imperialist state.[58] Other times they call it

[53] Haya de la Torre, *Y después de la guerra ¿qué?*, pp. 205–222.
[54] Manuel Seoane, "Where Do We Go From Here?," *Inter-American*, V (March, 1946), 24.
[55] *Plan de acción*, p. 11.
[56] Partido Aprista Peruano, Federación Aprista Juvenil, *op. cit.*, p. 5.
[57] El Buró de Redactores de "Cuaderno Aprista," *op. cit.*, p. 10.
[58] Seoane, *Nuestros fines*, p. 25; Haya de la Torre, "El estado antimperialista," *El antimperialismo y el Apra*, pp. 129–141; Saco, "El estado anti-imperialista," *Síntesis Aprista*, pp. 101–123.

functional democracy.[59] The Apristas define functional democracy as a political system in which the citizen has rights and duties as a citizen and also has rights and duties flowing from his participation in the economic life of the country. Functional democracy recognizes this dual role played by each person and, therefore, tries to create both economic and political democracy for all.[60]

Whatever name the new state will be known by, the ideas of the Apristas on the subject are clear. They say the new state would be based on the three oppressed and exploited groups in Peru: the workers, the farmers, and the middle class. The new state would have two enemies, the present feudal rulers of Peru and the foreign imperialists. It would try, however, to oppose its two enemies one at a time in order not to be crushed. The new state would do business with the foreign imperialists while, at the same time, it would try to destroy the economic power of the feudal landowning class.[61] This does not mean the Aprista state would be in favor of imperialism. Since the new state would represent the interests of the majority, the Apristas claim that it would be unable to neglect the interests it represented and would defend the nation from imperialism.[62]

The first thing to be done by the new state controlled by the Apristas would be to assemble statistical information about Peru, establish a national department of statistics, and hold a national economic congress.[63] This national economic congress would be the body which would work out the new economic program for Peru. It would be made up of representatives of all aspects of the economic life of the country: production, distribution, and consumption, and it would attempt to work out a realistic program for the development of the country.[64]

Along with the amassing of information and the planning by the national economic congress would come a decentralization of the government. Peru would be scientifically divided into regions based on economic reality. The division would be both political and economic.[65]

[59] Haya de la Torre, *Política Aprista,* p. 56.

[60] Partido Aprista Peruano, *El proceso Haya de la Torre* (1933), p. 39; El Buró de Redactores de "Cuaderno Aprista," *La verdad del aprismo* (1940), pp. 10–12.

[61] Haya de la Torre, *El antimperialismo y el Apra,* pp. 145–164.

[62] Haya de la Torre, "El rol del estado según el aprismo," *Política Aprista,* pp. 109–111; Fergac (ed.), *op. cit.,* p. 96.

[63] *Plan de acción,* p. 9. Haya de la Torre points out that the Kemmerer financial mission to Peru in 1930 had to prepare its program without having adequate information at its disposal. *Política Aprista,* p. 188; *supra,* p. 6, n. 20.

[64] Haya de la Torre, *Política Aprista,* pp. 105–107.

[65] "We who have always lived copying everything, have tried to adapt to our territory the French Departmental type of division which fits a homogeneous territory and economy very well but is very bad for our economic, social, and topographic

The Apristas maintain that this division is inevitable, because Peru has within its boundaries all stages of political and economic development from the lowest barbarism to a more or less elevated civilization. Peru, therefore, must have a multiform policy which takes its differences into account.[66] Each region must be given administrative and economic autonomy, and a harmonious relationship based on a division of labor must be worked out between the central government and the regions. The regional authorities would handle local matters and the central government would handle those matters which concern two or more regions and national matters. The regional officials would appoint their own employees, and the national authorities would be forbidden to interfere with their actions.[67]

The Apristas are proposing a form of federalism for Peru. The idea originates in their objection to the centralization that dictatorial government requires and in the role that Lima plays in Peruvian life. Seoane points out that Lima is an artificial creation, a product of the Spanish conquest. He claims that Lima's predominant mentality is colonial and conceited; and Lima thinks Lima is Peru. The Apristas, in opposition to this, call themselves anticentralists and demand self-government in local affairs for the regions of Peru.[68]

After the introduction of decentralization, the Apristas propose to strengthen the municipal governments. They would enlarge the field of activities of the local authorities and give them greater political, economic, and administrative power. The Apristas believe this would help to weaken the central government and would give democracy an experimental basis. The city would become a practical school of government.[69]

After the creation of regionalism, the character of the Peruvian Congress would change. The Apristas propose to make the Peruvian legislative body unicameral based on economic constituencies instead of the present bicameral body based on geographical constituencies. This is

---

conformation. Is the existence of departments in Peru (provinces in Chile and Argentina) not strange when they include the coast, the sierra, and the montaña, in each one of which the climate, the population, etc. are very different. By means of economic regionalism, the State will receive a new territorial demarcation which can be more in agreement with its various aspects. Each one of the regions created should be equal and have effective autonomy to be able to prevent the central power from absorbing the riches which each area should be able to create." Saco, *op. cit.*, p. 123.

[66] Fergac (ed.), *op. cit.*, pp. 19–21.

[67] Haya de la Torre, *Política Aprista*, pp. 9–10, 113–114.

[68] Seoane, "Nuestro anticentralismo," *Nuestros fines*, pp. 51–52; Haya de la Torre says, "The Peruvian Apristas are regionalists and anticentralists just as they are nationalists and democrats: NOT ONLY POLITICALLY BUT ECONOMICALLY." In Fergac (ed.), *op. cit.*, pp. 19–20.

[69] Haya de la Torre, *Política Aprista*, pp. 115–116.

another aspect of what they mean by functional democracy; having the legislature become a functional body representing the various regions and interests of the nation.[70] They think this would prevent the exclusively political direction of legislation and would prevent "malignant quackery, confused opportunism, the fantasy and the eagerness to apply the unadaptable to the country."[71]

PUBLIC ADMINISTRATION

An efficiently organized democratic state requires an administration composed of a permanent, specialized body of public employees chosen solely for merit. The Apristas propose the creation of this kind of administrative body for Peru. Entrance into the public service is to be based on examinations open to all. The Apristas pledge to oppose nepotism and favoritism in office, as well as all wasteful expenditures. They would give preference in hiring—when there is equality of ability—to those who lack private income and need to work to make a living.

To insure honesty within the public service the Apristas propose punishment for all who are delinquent in the discharge of their public duties. They would also promote honesty in public service by publicity. They advocate the compulsory filing of a personal financial statement by every elected and appointed public official before and after taking office. Each public official would be required to remain in Peru for a fixed period after leaving office. Honesty would also be fostered by the payment of bonuses to the lowest-paid public employees according to the number of children each employee supports.

To improve the functioning of the various departments of the administration the Apristas advocate the creation of a series of independent, technical, advisory committees to consult with the government departments. They suggest that the official organ of the government be turned into an educational organ which would have a monopoly on the publication of official information.[72]

The Apristas propose a merit system in the public service, not only to improve the quality of its work, but in order to weaken the power of the government, especially the power of the President. The Apristas contend that the President of Peru concentrates too much power in his hands by arbitrary control of the administration. A merit system would also give the public employees pride in their work and make them strive

[70] Fergac (ed.), *op. cit.*, pp. 80–87.
[71] Haya de la Torre, *Política Aprista*, p. 116.
[72] *Plan de acción*, pp. 12–14; Haya de la Torre, *Política Aprista*, p. 114.

to do better, for they would know that ability is the only road to advancement.[73]

The Aprista program suggests improving the administration by reorganizing the work of the central government. This could be done, according to the Apristas, by creating new ministries and by reorganizing some of the existing ministries.[74] Seoane pointed out in 1931 that because the government of Peru was constructed on a foreign model, after one hundred and ten years of independence it did not have a Ministry of Agriculture and Mines although Peru was primarily an agricultural and mining country.[75]

JUSTICE

The Apristas propose to reorganize the judicial power by giving it organic and economic autonomy and by providing an adequate salary scale for the functionaries and employees. They would establish police courts and extend the institution of the justice of the peace to all parts of the country. The Aprista program pledges a reduction of the cost of obtaining justice and a shortening of the judicial process. The Apristas propose to create a commission of lawyer specialists to make a study of the reform and codification of the laws.[76]

PERUVIAN FOREIGN RELATIONS

The section of the domestic program dealing with Peru's international relations begins with a promise to work for closer economic and intellectual coöperation among the Latin American peoples. It proposes toward that end the signing of commercial treaties, the holding of commercial congresses, the creation of a new Latin American organization to sponsor various meetings, interchange of students and teachers, and the creation of a Latin American continental citizenship. The Apristas say they would permit Peruvians who become naturalized in another country to keep their Peruvian citizenship. They advocate a defense pact among the Latin American nations to defend them from imperialism. They propose the formation of a Latin American arbitration tribunal. They end this section with a pledge to maintain friendly relations with all the countries of the world.[77]

[73] Haya de la Torre, *Política Aprista*, pp. 114–115.
[74] *Plan de acción*, p. 11.
[75] Seoane, *Páginas polémicas*, pp. 42–44.
[76] *Plan de acción*, p. 24. This is a subject that Aprista writings fail to discuss extensively.
[77] *Ibid.*, pp. 11–12.

ECONOMICS AND FINANCE

The Apristas have worked out a detailed program for the development of the Peruvian economy. In spite of the fact that they call themselves Socialists, they have always said that they do not want to institute immediate socialism. Rather they present their economic goal as that of securing economic independence for Peru. This idea is derived from their contention that the only realistic economic program for Peru must be one based on the reality of the country. Since the economic reality is completely different from that of Europe, Peru cannot take European socialism and introduce it into the country. Moreover, they say, Peru has never had the orderly economic development that Europe experienced—from barbarism to feudalism, to mercantilism, to a capitalist period, and finally to an industrial period. Peru, according to the Apristas, is a land where one can find all the stages of economic and social development of the world existing side by side. These include cannibalism, barbarism, feudalism, and modern imperialistic industrialism.[78]

The Apristas claim that the various kinds of economic development within Peru can be divided into two general categories: the native economy which is chiefly agricultural, backward, and geared to domestic consumption, and an international economy which is highly organized, technical, and geared to the world market.[79] The native economy produces for local consumption almost exclusively whereas the internationally controlled economy produces raw materials for the world market. The Aprista criticism of this arrangement is that Peru produces raw materials for the world market which are sold at low prices. Then Peru buys manufactured articles, in many cases made of Peruvian raw materials, at high prices. Another effect of this type of economy, according to the Apristas, is that, although Peru is primarily an agricultural country, she is unable to feed her population and must import rice, potatoes, and wheat, and other foodstuffs.[80]

Peru is sometimes referred to by the Apristas as an empty land waiting to be exploited. It has twice the area of France and one-fifth the population. It has land waiting to be irrigated, mines waiting to be exploited, a vast area in the Amazon valley which could become a new wonderland. All this is waiting, they say, for people with imagination

[78] Seoane, *Páginas polémicas*, pp. 72–74; Haya de la Torre, *Política Aprista*, pp. 41–42; Víctor Raúl Haya de la Torre, *Impresiones de la Inglaterra imperialista y la Rusia Soviética* (1932), pp. 134–135.

[79] Haya de la Torre, *Política Aprista*, p. 43.

[80] Seoane, *Páginas polémicas*, p. 37.

and courage who can forget the old selfish ways of doing things.[81] As Seoane puts it, "We have rich lands and poor men. And we have too much land and too few men. Put that way the economic solution seems simple. We must improve our production methods, raise the standard of living, and increase the average man's purchasing power so that he may take more part in international trade."[82] The Apristas say it is foolish to talk about redistributing the small amount of wealth there is in Peru. Rather they propose to create new wealth which the entire population can share. They would do this by beginning new enterprises and by creating a democratically planned society.[83]

As has been pointed out, as soon as the Apristas might control the Peruvian government they would set up a statistical agency and convene a national economic congress. When the information had been collected, Peru would then be able to begin to plan her future development. The Apristas never advocate the immediate socialization of the Peruvian economy; that is a very long-range objective. Haya de la Torre and Manuel Seoane use the term "state capitalism" to describe the Aprista goal.[84] They appear to prefer the organized intervention of the state in the economic life of the country, but they have never been too clear on exactly how the state would function to control the economy. In some respects their ideas are similar to those of the British Labour party, and some of their ideas resemble certain of the New Deal measures adopted in the United States. Although the Apristas have never been very exact in describing what they do want, they have been definite in describing what they do not want. The Aprista state intervention in the economy would not resemble technocracy, German or Italian fascism, or Soviet communism.[85] As can be seen from the specific proposals they make in the various fields of economic life, they visualize the state as taking an active part in planning, stimulating, and financing production. This would be accompanied by state ownership of certain important sectors of the economy and the development of coöperatively

[81] El Buró de Redactores de "Cuaderno Aprista," *40 preguntas y 40 respuestas*, pp. 26–27.

[82] "Where Do We Go From Here?," *Inter-American*, V, p. 23; the Apristas often quote Alexander Von Humboldt's remark that the people of Peru are "beggars seated on seats made of gold." Manuel Seoane, *Nuestra América y la guerra* (1940), p. 61.

[83] Seoane, "Where Do We Go From Here?," *Inter-American*, V, pp 23–25; Víctor Raúl Haya de la Torre, speech of May 20, 1945, reported in the *Peruvian Times*, June 1, 1945, p. 1.

[84] Haya de la Torre, *¿A dónde va Indoamérica?*, p. 259; Seoane, *Nuestros fines*, pp. 23, 27.

[85] Carlos Manuel Cox, *Dinámica económica del aprismo* (1948), pp. 31–34; Saco, *op. cit.*, pp. 107–110.

owned enterprises. Whether or not all this would add up to a socialist society depends upon the definition given to the word socialist.[86]

The attempt by the Apristas to put their economic ideas into practice when they had majority support in the Peruvian Congress from 1945 to 1948 illustrates their conception of economic organization. Certain legislation enacting part of the Aprista economic program into law was passed at that time either by one or both of the houses of Congress.

The two basic instruments the Apristas would use to set up their planned society are a national economic congress and a national financial corporation. Of these the congress is the most important proposal. A bill creating a national economic congress was approved by the Peruvian Chamber of Deputies on June 4, 1946.[87] This was no new proposal for the Apristas; it had appeared as the first paragraph of their plan for Peru adopted by the first national congress of the Peruvian Aprista party in August, 1931.[88]

The national economic congress, as described in the bill, would be an advisory agency which would accumulate information and develop technical plans for the future development of the country. If they approved, the executive and legislative bodies would put these plans into effect. The delegates to the economic congress would represent all segments of Peruvian society including the government, capital, labor, and the professions. Decisions would be reached by majority vote. The national economic congress would have four component parts: a permanent technical council, a biennial plenary assembly, an executive committee, and national or regional subcongresses.[89]

The congress and its agencies would do the economic planning for Peru. It would be up to the legislature and the President to turn the congress's plans into reality, but the Apristas see no difficulty here. They think that after a proposal has been studied and discussed by the varied elements which belong to the economic congress, and has received a majority vote, the political agencies would adopt the proposed plans. As the Apristas view its function, the national economic congress would determine what is being produced in Peru, what is being imported and exported, what could be produced for consumption and export, and on the basis of this information would suggest plans to improve the economy.[90]

The second arm of the proposed Aprista planned economy would be a national financial corporation. This organization would fit into a

---

[86] El Buró de Redactores de "Cuaderno Aprista," *La verdad del aprismo*, p. 9.
[87] This bill is reprinted in Cox, *op. cit.*, pp. 149–158.
[88] *Plan de acción*, p. 9.
[89] Cox, *op. cit.*, p. 150.
[90] *Ibid.*, p. 144.

planned society by financing the projects suggested by the economic congress and adopted by the political organs of the state. This organization would represent Peru in dealing with international financial organizations, such as the Export-Import Bank and the International Bank for Reconstruction and Development, and would act as the intermediary between the international banks and the various financial institutions in Peru.[91] The chief aim of the national financial corporation would be to finance the development of new enterprises. It would be an organization similar to the Reconstruction Finance Corporation of the United States or the Nacional Financiera, S.A. of Mexico.[92]

A third proposal put forward by the Apristas is that the state should foster the coöperative movement. Producer and consumer coöperatives would help put into effect some of the plans proposed by the national economic congress and would help meet the lack of capital in Peru. Since a coöperative gathers together small sums of money from a large number of people it would be able to find capital which could not be found in any other way and consequently be able to help finance enterprises that could not be financed otherwise. The Apristas suggest that the state create a central coöperative bank to supply credit to newly organized coöperative enterprises. Carlos Manuel Cox, in arguing for coöperatives in the Peruvian Chamber of Deputies, pointed out that the Scandinavian countries were able to improve their economic situation by fostering coöperatives. Peru, he stated, should imitate these small countries.[93]

The Apristas think that only after Peru has a government controlled by them, a national economic congress, and a national financial corporation functioning, and is following a policy of fostering coöperative organizations will it be ready to go ahead with the various points of their economic program. This program calls for stimulating agriculture, mining, industry, and commerce by providing them with state aid. The Apristas suggest that a protective tariff be set up to foster industrialization. Speculation by trusts should be prevented by legislation.[94] All monopolies granted to private parties should be annulled, and all contracts injurious to the national sovereignty should be canceled.[95] The

[91] *Ibid.*, pp. 43–44.

[92] *Ibid.*, pp. 52–55.

[93] *Ibid.*, pp. 22–24; El Buró de Redactores de "Cuaderno Aprista," *40 preguntas y 40 respuestas*, p. 8; Haya de la Torre, *Política Aprista*, pp. 112–113.

[94] *Plan de acción*, pp. 14–16.

[95] Manuel Seoane in 1931 gave an example of the kind of contract that should be canceled: the contract for the monopoly on matches in Peru. He pointed out that in Peru one paid ten centavos for a box of matches, whereas they were given away free with the purchase of a package of cigarettes in Argentina and other countries. *Páginas polémicas*, p. 79. Another monopoly opposed by the Apristas was that on salt. Cox, "El estanco de la sal," *op. cit.*, pp. 116–118.

Apristas would especially like to void the contract by which the Peruvian Corporation, a British company, obtained ownership of most of Peru's railroads in perpetuity. They believe that insurance and the means of transportation should be nationalized.[96]

The Apristas never wanted expropriation or nationalization of industry on a general basis.[97] When they talk about complete nationalization and socialization it is always a long-range aim. Even when they advocate nationalization they want it to be expropriation with compensation.[98] This is especially true of their attitude toward the nationalization of foreign-owned enterprises. Seoane, for example, argues that Peru is too weak to resist any force that an imperialist country might send to punish it for expropriating foreign property. Even more important than this, he asks, where could Peru get the technical competence to run the expropriated industries? Where would it sell the products of these industries if it learns to operate them? Suppose Peru expropriated the oil industry, would Standard Oil permit Peru to sell that oil on the world market; and further, where would Peru get tankers to transport the oil if it could be sold?[99] Seoane concludes that the most practical program for Peru would be to force foreign enterprises to pay good wages and adequate taxes. The tax funds could then be used to create protected industries whose purpose would be to produce those articles needed to improve life in Peru.[100]

Haya de la Torre expressed it another way. He said Peru needed foreign capital, but it had to be used in coöperation with the economic life of the country and within a plan established by the government. He compared Peru to a man getting a blood transfusion. Peru needed the foreign capital, but if it got more than it could assimilate it could be as harmful as too much blood to the man getting a transfusion.[101] "Aprismo cannot oppose the foreign capital that may come [to Peru]. We do not have capital with which to exploit our riches. What Aprismo desires is that foreign capital, which comes to Peru for its own needs, should be prepared to accept the conditions which other countries impose upon it. It should observe the national legislation, justly recompense the labor of the Peruvians, and contribute a just proportion to

[96] Seoane, *Nuestros fines*, pp. 48–50.

[97] Manuel Seoane, *Comunistas criollos* (1933), pp. 45–47.

[98] For example, their proposal to expropriate large estates so they could be used to produce those things needed for the internal market contained a promise to pay for them at a fair value. *Plan de acción*, p. 17.

[99] One is impressed with Seoane's reasoning in light of the predicament in which Iran finds itself in 1952 as a result of expropriating its foreign-owned oil enterprise.

[100] Seoane, *Páginas polémicas*, pp. 75–80.

[101] In Mario de Bernaschina, "Entrevista con Haya de la Torre," *Revista de América* (1943), p. 79.

the revenue of the government. This simple nationalist ambition leads us to demand the priority of our sovereignty, constantly treated with contempt until now, and the establishment of a regime where the needs of the country and foreign capitalism are reflected in a system of mutual rewards."[102]

In the financial program, the Apristas propose a radical reform of the tax system. Among the specific suggestions are the abolition of indirect taxes and the creation of a system of direct taxes on inheritance, gifts, legacies, and income. They propose progressive taxes on income based on its source and its destination. They recommend heavy taxes on luxuries and idle capital. They advocate reforming the tariff legislation. Another proposal is that the national debt be reorganized and that a stable currency be maintained. They suggest that the state control and restrict the export of capital and regulate foreign investments and profits. They believe that the consular organization should be improved. They would sponsor thrift among workers and place all pawnshops under municipal ownership. The final plank in the Aprista financial program proposes a scientific budget for the nation with a regular part allotted to the exploitation of the national riches.[103]

AGRICULTURE

Agriculture is basic to the economy of Peru; hence the Apristas would have the government give especial attention to its problems.[104] Alfredo Saco, one of the Aprista leaders, maintains that this is necessary because for a long time Peru has concentrated on the production of export crops for a world market, neglecting the production of food crops for domestic consumption.[105] To correct the situation the Apristas suggested an agricultural program in the 1931 *Plan de acción*.[106] Saco, writing in 1946, thought this program was still the best proposal yet made to solve Peru's agricultural problems.[107]

The Aprista agricultural program contains five parts, as follows:

1. National and social agrarian policy
2. Policy for agricultural production
3. Policy for improvement and colonization
4. Policy for agricultural education
5. Agrarian public administration[108]

---

[102] Manuel Seoane, *Las calumnias contra el aprismo*, quoted in Saco, *op. cit.*, p. 118.
[103] *Plan de acción*, pp. 14–16.
[104] *Ibid.*, p. 16; Alfredo Saco, *Programa agrario del aprismo* (1946), p. 13.
[105] Saco, *Programa agrario del aprismo*, p. 7.
[106] *Plan de acción*, pp. 16–18.
[107] Saco, *Programa agrario del aprismo*, p. 8.
[108] *Ibid.*, p. 11.

These five points, the Apristas maintain, contain practically all that is needed for a complete agricultural policy for Peru. A national policy is needed to defend the country from the actions of foreign capitalism; a social policy is needed to improve the life of the rural masses; a production policy is needed to guide the development of agriculture; a policy of improvement and colonization is needed to increase the area under cultivation and to increase the population; an educational policy is needed to give technical knowledge to the farmers; and an administrative reorganization is needed to make the government capable of handling the necessary work.[109]

It is impossible to control a country when the great majority of the population do not own and control the land, and when the foreign owner is not strictly controlled. The Apristas agree with Ramsay MacDonald's statement that what socialism wants is not to abolish private property but to diffuse it. Since Peru is primarily an agricultural country, the Apristas would place especial attention on the agrarian problem to achieve that aim.[110]

The Apristas claim that to control imperialistic penetration into agriculture the government must have the power to regulate the purchase and sale of large land holdings. Large farms should keep records of their operations, and the government must have the power to inspect agricultural businesses when necessary. These powers are needed to prevent the sale of land to foreigners when it is harmful to the national interest; it is needed because the desire for large profits leads some people to alienate the land to any one who pays a high price. Foreign capital, according to Saco, enters Peru through the large estate.[111]

To solve the problem of imperialistic penetration into agriculture the Apristas propose the incorporation of the Indian into the national life. The Indian now lives in Peru, but on a level where he is almost completely removed from national production and consumption; he lives on a subsistence level. The Apristas desire to transform him into a modern man. Some say that this cannot be done because the Indian is lazy, torpid, and without ambition. But evidence offered by the civilized Indian today demonstrates to Saco that actually the mass of the Indians have been offering passive resistance (*huelga de brazos caídos*), ever since the Spanish conquest, to the abuses they have suffered and to the lack of understanding of their problems by the government. The Indian is introverted, Saco writes, and hides the genius which created the Inca

[109] *Ibid.*, p. 12.
[110] *Ibid.*, pp. 12–13.
[111] *Ibid.*, pp. 14–15.

Empire. Saco does not think the problem can be solved easily or that one can make the Indian into something foreign to his nature. By taking into account his psychological and biological characteristics as well as the economic situation, a solution can be worked out that is suitable to the Indian.[112]

The problem of integrating the Indian into Peruvian life, according to Saco, is closely connected with his demand for land. A large proportion of the Indian population owns no land, and the small section which does own land usually works it in a primitive manner. The Indian's need for land can be met by enlarging the area owned by the present Indian communities and by created new communities. At the same time the Indian must be taught modern methods of cultivation to increase the yield from his fields.[113] The Aprista *Plan de acción* promises legislation designed to conserve and modernize the indigenous community.[114] To carry out their ideas about modernizing the Indian communities the Apristas in 1931 proposed the following measures: (1) the creation of a Bureau of Indian Affairs; (2) the naming of commissions to solve boundary disputes; (3) the evaluation and the census of community property; (4) the survey and the setting of land marks on all Indian communities; (5) the revision of the property titles of the presumed usurpers of communal goods; and (6) the expropriation of estates adjacent to communal property when, in the judgment of the government, it may be necessary to give the Indian sufficient land. Some of these proposals made in 1931 have been enacted into law, but, according to Saco, not enough has been done.[115]

[112] *Ibid.*, pp. 15–17.

[113] *Ibid.*, p. 18.

[114] *Plan de acción*, p. 23. This aspect of the Aprista program is incorporated in the 1933 Constitution of Peru. Alfredo Saco points to this section as a step in the right direction although he claims that these provisions will remain a "dead letter" until such time as a government interested in the Indian comes to power. Saco, *Programa agrario del aprismo*, p. 18. The Constitution reads as follows:

"Art. 207. The Indian communities have legal existence and juridical personality.

"Art. 208. The State guarantees the integrity of the property of these communities.

"Art. 209. The property of these communities is imprescriptible and inalienable, except in case of expropriation for reasons of public utility, with prior indemnification. Such property is likewise unattachable.

"Art. 210. Neither the municipal councils nor any body or authority shall intervene in the collection or in the administration of the revenues and goods of the communities.

"Art. 211. The State shall give preference in apportioning lands to the Indian communities that may not have them in sufficient amount for the necessities of their populations, and may expropriate lands under private ownership for this purpose, with prior indemnification.

"Art. 212. The State shall enact the civil, penal, economic, educational, and administrative legislation that the peculiar conditions of the Indians may require."

[115] Saco, *Programa agrario del aprismo*, pp. 18–19.

Since the Apristas advocate coöperatives, they believe this technique could be adopted by the Indian community. The exact form of the coöperatives would depend upon local conditions, but they would consist of a combination of the old Indian communal organizations with the techniques of modern coöperatives. In certain types of agriculture (fruit growing, flower growing) the Apristas recommend individual landowning, but in most cases they propose collective ownership with the profits divided among all members of the coöperatives.[116] The Apristas do not suggest confiscating property in order to begin the agricultural coöperatives. They would obtain land for this purpose from the following sources: using land owned by the government; having the state buy indebted land; leasing land from proprietors; and expropriating—with compensation—land that is kept idle or partly idle. The budget should annually provide funds for this purpose.[117]

With regard to the small farmers, the Apristas want the government to regulate the contracts between the proprietors and the Indians bound to service (*yanacones*) and the tenant farmers (*subarrendatarios o copartícipes*).[118] They think intermediaries and high interest rates should be eliminated. The Apristas propose that all laws dealing with working conditions apply to farm workers.[119]

To create a policy for agricultural production the Apristas propose a study be made of the economy of Peru. Once information is available then technical improvement can begin. At present technical improvement is held back by the feudal organization of society; yet only by technical improvement can the standard of living be raised. In order to improve production the Apristas propose state aid to agriculture consisting of market and technical information and economic aid when necessary. Economic aid is necessary, according to the Apristas, because the small farmers do not have the resources needed to obtain new seeds and selected breeds of cattle and to finance other proposed measures.[120]

The Apristas advocate a system of government credit for farmers.

---

[116] *Ibid.*, pp. 19–21. This insistence by the Apristas upon the need for strengthening the Indian communities and introducing coöperative methods of agricultural work leads some of their opponents to call them "Communist." One of the anonymous pamphlets issued to fight Aprismo makes the claim that individual ownership is the true solution for Peru and that the Indian community is really a form of individual ownership. This pamphlet states that there is no communal tradition in Peru and the only result of any attempt to start coöperative agriculture would resemble Russian forced labor or collective farms. See *El verdadero plan de la Alianza Popular Revolucionaria Americana*, Editorial Pachacutek (no author or date).

[117] Saco, *Programa agrario del aprismo*, pp. 21–22.

[118] The Apristas organized an agricultural coöperative, Santa Rosa, which was very successful from 1931 to 1933 in helping the *yanacones* until the rich landowners decided it was communism and destroyed it. *Ibid.*, pp. 23–24.

[119] *Ibid.*, pp. 25–27.

[120] *Ibid.*, pp. 30–31.

There has been an agricultural bank in Peru since 1929, but Saco claims that because of the manner in which the law creating the bank was written and because of the character of the government, the bank has used its funds to aid large industrial agricultural enterprises and not the small farmer.[121] The Apristas would have a governmental bank created solely for the purpose of supplying credit to small farmers.[122]

Two planks from the program on economics and finance would aid agriculture: the creation of a new national bank and of coöperative organizations for supplying credit for production and consumption. The Apristas would have the new credit organizations lend seed and machinery in addition to money. Regional stations might be created to lend farm machinery and equipment to the small Indian farmers at a moderate rental payable after harvest.[123]

The Apristas think it is impossible for Peru to lose its colonial character and become an organized country without producing its own bread, milk, eggs, meat, and vegetables. The government, they insist, must stop the anarchy in production and direct it to produce what the country needs to feed, clothe, and shelter its people before it produces raw materials such as cotton and sugar for the world market. The decision as to what is to be grown cannot be left to the individual. The Apristas think the ideal situation would be a world organization of production or at least an inter-American organization, but until such time as production is organized internationally, Peru must control it in her own country. This control should aim at the diversification and the improvement of agricultural production.[124] Other measures which would help production would be the establishment of economic regionalism in Peru; the establishment of agricultural extension stations; the organization of social security for farmers; and the electrification of Peru to supply power and irrigation water.[125]

The Apristas make several proposals to improve agriculture and to colonize the country. They claim that Peru is not a worn-out area, but a new land waiting for its development. They state that the Inca Empire had more land under cultivation and supported a larger population than present-day Peru.[126] There is no reason, they say, why modern Peru

[121] *Ibid.*, pp. 31–32.

[122] The Apristas think Peru could imitate Mexico's *Ley de Crédito Agrícola de México* and its *Banco Nacional de Crédito Ejidal. Ibid.*, p. 32.

[123] *Ibid.*, p. 33.

[124] *Ibid.*, pp. 34–36.

[125] *Ibid.*, pp. 36–38.

[126] Philip Ainsworth Means, a student of Inca life, came to the same conclusion. He estimated in 1931 that the population of the Inca Empire was approximately twice what it was in the same area at the time Means was writing. *Ancient Civilizations of the Andes* (1931), p. 296.

cannot increase its area under cultivation and its population. To achieve this aim they propose the following measures: irrigate more land, drain certain areas, fertilize the soil, regulate the flow of streams, prevent floods, build canals, clear the forests in the montaña, build rural highways, and preserve the fertility of the soil now under cultivation. An important step would be the colonization of the montaña. This would have to be carefully planned and probably would require immigrants from outside Peru.[127]

The Apristas suggest that agriculture should be taught in all primary schools. At the same time they propose that special primary, secondary, and university agricultural schools be created. The philosophy of the coöperative movement should be taught by the schools to enable farm youth to learn to work together.[128]

To improve the administration of agriculture the Apristas suggest the creation of technical advisory bodies to aid the ministry. They also suggest a reorganization of the Ministry of Agriculture. They point out that although Peru is primarily an agricultural country it was not until January, 1943, that a Ministry of Agriculture was set up. Finally, the Apristas insist that in addition to laws and principles Peru needs a new group of ministers—Apristas.[129]

THE REDEMPTION OF THE INDIAN

The Apristas put the redemption of the Indian in the forefront of their program.[130] They view the Indians as an alien body living alongside the rest of the Peruvian population, but not sharing the life of the country. Further, they see the Indians as an oppressed class which must be freed if Peru is ever to progress because the Indians comprise the majority of the population.[131] The problem is primarily economic and not one of race or color.[132] They maintain that not all Indians are exploited and not all those exploited are Indians. The Apristas desire social justice for all Peruvians, hence they see the need for defending the Indian as they defend all who are exploited.[133]

The root of the problem, according to the Apristas, is how to incorporate the Indian into the life of the country. They claim that if the

[127] Saco, *Programa agrario del aprismo*, pp. 39–52.
[128] *Ibid.*, pp. 53–57.
[129] *Ibid.*, pp. 58–61.
[130] Víctor Raúl Haya de la Torre, "El problema del Indio," *Construyendo el aprismo* (1933), pp. 104–113.
[131] Cossio del Pomar, *op. cit.*, pp. 219–220; Seoane, *Nuestros fines*, pp. 31–33.
[132] Sánchez, *Carta a una indoamericana*, pp. 31–33.
[133] Seoane, *Nuestros fines*, pp. 33–34.

Indian is kept uneducated and living in poverty and filth, he will never be able to contribute much to Peru. If the state intervenes to educate him and improve his standard of living he will become a producer and a consumer and be able to contribute to the creation of a better Peru. The Apristas maintain they are not proposing such action because the Indian is Indian, but because the Indians form the exploited majority of the Peruvian population.[134] Since the majority of the population is rural, they insist the problem revolves around the Indians' need for land.[135]

The Apristas claim that after four hundred years of struggle between the Indian system of landowning, the ayllu, and the Spanish system, the latifundia, the ayllu still exists; it is an economic and social cell to which the Indians cling. The way to redeem the Indian, say the Apristas, is to maintain this ancient structure and provide modern techniques for it. The Apristas propose to make the ayllu the base of an Indian coöperative organization. With the creation of this organization there would be developed an educational and cultural program for the Indian.[136] This is imperative because the feudal domination of the Peruvian landowning class is paralleled in the intellectual servitude imposed on the Indian by the owner and priest. The redemption of the Indian, therefore, must be spiritual and educational as well as economic. Seoane pointed out in 1930 that there were 4,100 religious buildings in Peru and only 3,500 primary schools.[137] On another occasion, he stated that the Apristas hoped to set up a school facing every church.[138]

The educational program the Apristas propose for the Indian is not to be the European urban routine of other Peruvian schools or that of the barracks, but rather a new kind of school which they call the "Rural School." They point out that in the past a school was a place where an Indian child was taught to read and write to some degree. Then the child went home to live in a community where there was nothing to read and his little knowledge was soon forgotten. The rural schools envisioned by the Apristas would prepare the Indian child for life in the modern world. The child of a farmer would be taught those things which would help make him a better farmer. The child would be given a new conception of life, he would be taught personal hygiene, how to improve his agricultural methods, and how to fit himself into the economy of the region and of the country. He would be taught physical welfare and

[134] Haya de la Torre, *Y después de la guerra ¿qué?*, pp. 201–202.
[135] Cossio del Pomar, *op. cit.*, p. 220.
[136] Mario de Bernaschina, *op. cit.*, p. 80.
[137] Seoane, *Nuestros fines*, p. 36.
[138] Seoane, *Comunistas criollos*, p. 36.

spiritual pleasure. Reading and writing would be taught, but in relation to the life the child understands.[139]

In section nine of *Plan de acción,* the Apristas present their program for the redemption of the Indian in a systematic form. The main point, of course, is the incorporation of the Indian into the life of the country. This is to be done by various means including the conservation and modernization of the Indian community and special aid by the government to the smaller landowner. Within a general plan and the unifying influence of education the Apristas promise to respect the peculiarities of each Indian region. For the education of the Indian, the Apristas suggest that Indian teachers be used in the rural schools and that the Indian be taught in his own language as well as in Spanish. The Apristas recommend the stimulation of small Indian industries and native art and the introduction of agricultural coöperatives. They propose an energetic campaign against the abuses of alcohol and coca.[140] To insure that the government handles Indian affairs properly the Apristas propose that within each ministry a special section be created for handling the affairs of the indigenous population.[141]

Because of their emphasis on Indian problems, the Apristas often have been accused of being Indian nationalists or racists.[142] To this charge they reply that the critics who call them racists simply refuse to understand what the Apristas are trying to do. They answer the question, "Does the Aprista Party invoke an anti-white extreme Indian nationalism?" by saying:

> It is one of the many lies that the plutocratic reaction has thrown against Aprismo. Our Party cannot seek a retrogression of history nor an elimination of all that is not Indian in Peru. We aspire to the material and spiritual reincorporation of the Indian in the national life, and to the reappearance of the eternal virtues of the Peruvian race, the virtues of the Empire which were the inspiration of its social justice, of its moral grandeur, of its material progress, and of its energetic and creative leadership. We do not renounce European culture nor the contribution which the whites have brought to our soil. But we repudiate the colonial mentality which until now has

[139] Cossio del Pomar, *op. cit.*, p. 233; Magda Portal, "La escuela rural en el Perú," *Sayari*, II (Nov., 1946), 21–22.

[140] *Plan de acción*, p. 23.

[141] *Ibid.*, p. 11; it was not until June 24, 1938, that a Dirección de Asuntos Indígenas was created by decree. Saco, *op. cit.*, p. 19.

[142] William G. Fletcher, "Aprismo Today: an Explanation and a Critique," *Inter-American Quarterly*, vol. 3 (Oct., 1941), 17; Nicholas John Spykman, *America's Strategy in World Politics* (1942), p. 229. One critic goes so far as to say that one of the Apristas' basic purposes is "the developing and sustaining of a native culture purely Indian in character, devoid of all features and roots that might be considered Hispanic. The latter explains the hispanophobia rooted in the movement and revealed by Professor Sánchez' assertion." A. M. Méndez, "Letter to the editor," *Inter-American*, IV (March, 1945), 48.

adopted the anti-Peruvian attitude of scorning the Indians and whatever is Indian. We believe that a Peru should rise which assimilates within its new national features what is ethnically and culturally modern, uniting it with what is permanent in the imperial traditions. Then just as the new Peru is hybrid in race so it will be hybrid as a result of what is great in its three previous historical stages.[143]

EDUCATION

Closely related to the problem of the Indian is the general problem of education in Peru. The Apristas have always been keenly interested in education, probably because their movement began as a student organization. The Universidad Popular González Prada was set up by the students in the early 1920's for the purpose of bringing education to the workers who could not attend the regular schools. The college students taught regular classes and conducted a campaign against alcohol and in favor of sanitation.[144] Ever since that time, the Apristas considered their movement as educational in purpose even though it developed into a political party. Haya de la Torre, the jefe of the Aprista movement, was a teacher in the Anglo-Peruvian College in Lima at the time of his first expulsion from Peru by the dictatorship, and he has looked upon himself as a teacher ever since.[145] Haya told the author that this fundamental point of Aprista ideology could be summed up in the Aprista slogan: "Every one who knows, teach; every one who does not, study. If every one does that regularly success will come."[146]

The leaders of the movement believe that each individual is entitled to free education by the state to the limits of his capacities.[147] They propose that the Peruvian educational system be completely reorganized to make this possible. They maintain that reorganization is needed because "the great majority of the primary schools still are in the Paleolithic age."[148] They think this backwardness is a direct result of the domination of Peruvian society by the landowners. They claim the Peruvian landowners oppose education because they fear the education of their farm labor might endanger their position. To correct the situation the Apristas propose the creation of a complete system of various kinds of new schools and libraries—particularly, special agricultural

[143] El Buró de Redactores de "Cuaderno Aprista," *40 preguntas y 40 respuestas*, p. 28.

[144] *Almanaque la tribuna 1948*, pp. 183–184.

[145] John A. Mackay, *The Other Spanish Christ* (1933), p. 243.

[146] Personal interview, Los Angeles, California, April 1, 1948; the Apristas' Lima newspaper, *La tribuna*, for May 1, 1947, p. 3, gives the slogan in this way: "An Aprista always prepares himself to learn if he knows little and to teach if he knows much."

[147] *Plan de acción*, p. 10.

[148] Seoane, *Nuestros fines*, p. 36.

schools—and they wish to foster agricultural education in all schools. They suggest that a high percentage of the national income be used for education, especially to increase the pay of teachers. The *Plan de acción* also proposes special rates for students who use the transportation system and more physical education for students.[149]

The Apristas favor education becoming a monopoly of the state and separated from all Church control. This would be the only way, according to Seoane, to guarantee that the educational system is impartial and uniform. Furthermore, Seoane writes, if the children of all classes attend the same school system they would learn that all persons are equal before the Law, and the absurd and medieval prejudices of superiority which are accumulated in the private schools would disappear.[150]

LABOR

The Apristas advocate legislation which would give Peruvian workers many of the conditions enjoyed by workers in the most advanced countries. These proposals include an eight-hour day, with limited exceptions; one day of rest after six days of work; seven to fifteen days of paid annual vacation; a six-hour maximum working day for those less than sixteen years of age; a seven-hour maximum for night work and for those who work underground or in noxious industries; the prohibition of night work or dangerous or unhealthy work to those less than sixteen years of age and those older if they are not in perfect health. Also included in the plans for labor are minimum wages; obedience to labor laws by employers; minimum and maximum retirement pensions; and municipal employment offices.

The Apristas propose that employers supply at least a minimum of housing, schools, sanitary services, and hospitals for their workers. For women, they suggest equal pay for equal work and a paid rest period before and after childbirth. They believe that at least eighty per cent of the workers in a foreign enterprise should be Peruvian. They propose the creation of an organization to help workers adjust to industrial life.[151] The Apristas promise legislation which will punish those who utilize a person's labor without paying for it, particularly those who violate the laws protecting Indian women and children. They advocate a system of social security to protect the working population from the vicissitudes of life. Social security would be given free to all workers whose wages fall below a certain minimum.[152]

---

[149] *Plan de acción*, pp. 22–23.
[150] Seoane, *Nuestros fines*, pp. 37–38.
[151] *Plan de acción*, pp. 20–21; see also the discussion of wages and working hours in Luis E. Heysen, *Verdades de a puño* (1947), pp. 15–16.
[152] *Plan de acción*, p. 10.

The leaders of the Aprista movement have always tried to stimulate the creation of trade unions both to help the workers improve their conditions and to help create the new society envisioned by the Apristas.[153] They think unions have an important role to play in society and, therefore, try to stimulate their participation in the political life of the nation. The Apristas think trade unions should study problems facing the nation and participate in national and local elections. The unions should try to be all-inclusive, accepting into their ranks all workers regardless of their political ideas, religious creeds, race, or nationality. Such unions, say the Apristas, would be basic pillars of the new social order of the future.[154]

The trade-union activity of the Apristas culminated when they co-operated with trade-union groups in other countries to create the Inter-American Confederation of Labor. This organization was created at a conference held in Lima, Peru, from January 10 to January 13, 1948. Apristas were active in the work of the conference and one of the Aprista leaders, Arturo Sabroso Montoya, was elected vice-president of the new organization. The conference was attended by delegates representing trade unions in Bolivia, Brazil, Chile, Colombia, Costa Rica, the Dominican Republic, Dutch Guiana, Ecuador, El Salvador, Mexico, Peru, Puerto Rico, the United States of America (A. F. of L.), and Venezuela. The purpose of the conference was to create an inter-American labor organization which would be able to help the trade unions in the various countries. Most of the labor organizations represented at the conference had previously been members of the Confederación de Trabajadores de América Latina (C.T.A.L.) led by Vicente Lombardo Toledano. The Inter-American Confederation of Labor maintained that the C.T.A.L. and Lombardo Toledano were dominated by the Russian government and should be opposed by all workers.[155]

The Aprista movement and the trade unions influenced by its members were the only supporters of the new Inter-American Confederation

---

[153] See resolution on union organization in *Resoluciones de la convención de dirigentes del Partido Aprista Peruano, reunida en Lima, Perú, 1942* (1942), p. 10.

[154] Justo Enrique Debarbieri, "Discusión de los objectivos de la lucha sindical," in Guillermo Carnero Hoke and Ricardo Tello N. (eds.), *Informes humanes* (1945), pp. 60–63.

[155] Arturo Sabroso Montoya, "Hechos y razones que determinaron nuestra separación de la C.T.A.L.," *La tribuna,* Jan. 6, 1948, p. 7; Jan. 8, 1948, p. 8; Jan. 10, 1948, p. 8. The Apristas have always been opposed to the Communist movement in Latin America for many reasons. One of the reasons that Haya de la Torre has given for the Aprista opposition to the Communists in Latin America was that "Communism proposes 'permanent agitation' among the workers in the extractive industries in order to obstruct production and help the development of similar industries in Russia. Latin American sugar, cotton, petroleum, and other products compete in the world market

of Labor in Peru. The Apristas supported the new organization because its trade-union policy was similar to their own and because inter-American coöperation fitted in with Aprista ideas.[156] The conference in Lima and the new trade-union organization created there were attacked by various elements including the Communists in Peru, the Peronista trade unions in Argentina, and the Peruvian government. The opposition to the conference included a street demonstration organized by anti-Aprista groups in Lima. After the conference was over the government of Peru refused to allow the new organization to set up its headquarters in Lima.[157]

The Declaration of Principles of the Inter-American Confederation of Labor illustrates the Aprista point of view on labor problems. It read as follows:

1. The Inter-American Confederation of Labor has as its primary objective the organization of the manual and intellectual workers of American countries, without distinction of political or religious creeds, nationality, sex, color, or age, for struggle against the exploitation of man by man until the arrival of the emancipation.

2. In the struggle between capital and labor, the Inter-American Confederation of Labor will develop its action, inspired by the principles and methods of the class comprising the democratic labor movement, independent of all state tutelage or of totalitarian practices.

3. The laboring class should organize internationally.

4. As a first step towards this organization, the Inter-American Confederation of Labor will endeavor to strengthen the union organization of the laboring masses of democratic tendencies in the countries of America and will maintain fraternal relations, with all union organizations of the rest of the world who profess similar principles.

5. Within these postulates, the Inter-American Confederation of Labor will participate resolutely in all of the struggles of the laboring class until they are liberated from all forms of oppression and exploitation.[158]

---

with the Russian products. To contribute to their non-production in countries like ours, is to help Russian production. For even though we know that all these industries in Peru belong almost completely to foreigners and leave very little in Peru, we should take into account that the immediate result of the Communist plan will be the misery of our working population, without any immediate prospect of improvement since they are not prepared to control production and govern the State themselves, as we have demonstrated." Haya de la Torre, *Impressiones de la Inglaterra imperialista y la Rusia Soviética*, pp. 127–128.

[156] See the editorial in *La tribuna*, Jan. 10, 1948, p. 4.

[157] *La tribuna*, Jan. 3, 1948, p. 3; Jan. 6, 1948, p. 7; Jan. 8, 1948, p. 8; Jan. 10, 1948, pp. 1, 6–9; Jan. 11, 1948, pp. 1, 4, 6–7; *Peruvian Times*, Jan. 2, 1948, p. 1; Jan. 9, 1948, p. 2; Jan. 16–23, 1948, p. 1; Jan. 30, 1948, p. 1 supplement; Feb. 6, 1948, pp. 9, 12. For a Communist view of this new organization and of the Apristas, see: *Conclusiones y resoluciones de la Primera Conferencia Obrera Regional del Sur* (1947). This pamphlet defends the Confederación de Trabajadores de América Latina and Vicente Lombardo Toledano; denies they are Communist and receive orders from Moscow, and accuses the American Federation of Labor and the Aprista movement of being agents of Yankee imperialism.

[158] *Peruvian Times*, Jan. 9, 1948, p. 2.

HYGIENE AND SOCIAL ASSISTANCE

In the field of hygiene and social assistance the Apristas propose to reorganize and intensify the struggle against malaria, tuberculosis, syphilis and other venereal diseases, leprosy, and cancer. They propose the creation of a national institution, with regional branches, to carry on the struggle against epidemics and to study the various diseases. They suggest the creation of regional hospitals, health resorts, dispensaries, sanitariums, and mental health clinics. They believe a campaign against alcoholism should be organized.

The Apristas propose to improve the Ministry of Hygiene and incorporate within it all of the societies of public welfare keeping as many of the present technical-administrative personnel of these societies as the service requires. They want legislation to protect children. They propose to promote sanitation for the whole population by stimulating the formation of a sanitary conscience in the country. The Apristas desire to increase the medical personnel and the dental services of the state. They advocate the improvement of the profession of pharmacy and the creation of a Peruvian pharmacopoeia. The program recommends making the sale of narcotics a state monopoly.[159]

PUBLIC WORKS

In the field of public works the Apristas propose to revise the system so that all projects would be planned by the government and carried out after public bidding. They propose the creation of technical regional councils for public works and the organization of coöperative organizations in which the government would participate for the construction of public projects. They would revise the fares on railroads and toll bridges in order to make them economically just and payable only in Peruvian currency.

They propose that a study be made to plan for the creation of a highway system to serve both local and regional needs. They advocate the construction of many cheap highways instead of only a few good, expensive roads. They suggest that all highways in Peru be declared public roads. They propose the construction of public works to provide water and drainage. They want laws to guide the planned development of the cities.[160]

MINING

The Aprista domestic program for mining is similar to the program for agriculture in that it proposes to assist the mining industry by supply-

[159] *Plan de acción*, pp. 24–25.
[160] *Ibid.*, pp. 25–26.

ing it with market and technical information and rendering it economic and legal aid by the state. Mining is one field in which the Apristas demand nationalization as soon as possible with the immediate nationalization of the vanadium and gold mines. The program advocates legislation requiring a fixed percentage of all mining profits to be invested either in the creation of new industries or in national-bank stock. The Apristas would set time limits on all mineral concessions.

The Apristas propose that a study be made of the practicability of establishing a silver-refining plant and the possibility of utilizing this metal in industry. They believe it is necessary to develop the mining of coal and to create a petroleum refinery in order to lower the cost of gasoline. They recommend coöperatives in the mining industry and the creation of central smelters to which minerals can be sent for processing. They suggest that those in control of large water-power enterprises be forced to sell a part of their generated power to the operators of small mines. They propose that the operators of reduction works be forced to handle at prices fixed by the state the minerals produced by small mining enterprises.[161]

IMMIGRATION

The Apristas want a plan of scientific colonization of the eastern montaña; at the same time they are opposed to the kind of immigration practiced by the Japanese in Peru. Their objection is based on the fact that the Japanese settle in groups, isolate themselves from the life of Peru, send their children to Japanese schools, and continue to speak Japanese. The Apristas, therefore, oppose Japanese mass immigration and want restrictions on the sale of land to the Japanese.[162] On the other hand, they want Peru to be hospitable to "those who came to Peru to work and to submit themselves to our laws, to learn our language, and to live our life and help the national progress and welfare."[163] As a result of this opinion the Apristas advocate the prevention of immigration to the coast and to the sierra until a plan could be worked out for the promotion of immigration which would have a cultural affinity to the Peruvian population and would be economically valuable to the country.[164]

THE ARMED FORCES

The Aprista program pledges to remove politics from the armed forces and to remove the influence of the armed forces from politics. The military personnel are to become a part of a technical organization

[161] *Ibid.*, pp. 18–20.

[162] Saco, *Programa agrario del aprismo*, pp. 13–14.

[163] El Buró de Redactores de "Cuaderno Aprista," *40 preguntas y 40 respuestas*, p. 7.

[164] *Plan de acción*, pp. 26–27.

dedicated to defending the honor and integrity of the nation and to upholding the rule of law. The Apristas claim that their organization is not an enemy of the Army, but rather is one that would transform the Army into a career service which would play a worth-while role within the new Peru. They propose to make military service generally obligatory. A council of defense would be set up to advise the executive about military affairs. All promotions would be handled by the council of defense with no outside interference from any source.

One of the novel ideas advanced by the Apristas is that the armed forces can become a mechanism to help incorporate the Indians into the life of the nation. This could be done by taking Indians into the armed forces and training them in such a way that they would return to their homes after military service with new ideas. To accomplish this end, the Apristas propose the construction of comfortable, hygienic barracks containing elementary schools. The Army could also aid the nation by creating military colonies in the montaña which would begin the development of that area. Military personnel aided by teachers, engineers, agricultural experts, and industrialists could scientifically develop the montaña. Battalions should be set up to construct roads and railroads. The Indians recruited into the Army who participate in this work would learn about machinery and modern methods of production. The Apristas propose that each recruit receive a discharge bonus of at least 100 soles for each year of military service.

The efficiency of the police department can be increased, the Apristas believe, through promotions by merit. They suggest the establishment of a military port complete with technical defenses, docks, arsenals, and workshops to serve as a base for the war and merchant fleets. They desire the efficient organization of the Merchant Marine, the hydrographical service, and the customs service. They propose a reform of the organic law of the Navy; and the repair and modernization of the fleet. Other proposals are to give the military personnel specialist training including sending them overseas for technical education; give the military personnel the benefits of social security; make the air corps independent; and increase the number of air lines in order to give all parts of the country their benefits.[165]

The Aprista Movement and the Church

The Aprista minimum program states, "We will separate the Church from the State and we will guarantee the neutrality of the State in

[165] *Ibid.*, pp. 27–29; El Buró de Redactores de "Cuaderno Aprista," *40 preguntas y 40 respuestas*, p. 9; Haya de la Torre, *Política Aprista*, pp. 59–62, 154–155; Partido Aprista Peruano, *El proceso Haya de la Torre*, pp. xxiv–xxvi.

religious subjects."[166] This is one of the most controversial changes advocated by the Apristas because Peru has always had an established Church which has had a very close connection with the government.[167] The Aprista proposal to separate Church and State, therefore, is opposed vigorously by a section of the Church and by certain sections of Peruvian public opinion which charge that Aprismo is an antireligious movement.

Luis Alberto Sánchez writes that the chief argument used to prove that the Aprista movement is antireligious is based on faulty reasoning. The argument goes as follows: Aprismo is a Marxist organization; Marxism is antireligious; therefore, Aprismo is also antireligious.[168] Sánchez claims that this reasoning is completely false, for Marxism is not an antireligious movement. Rather it is a philosophy of history which tries to deal with the economic organization of society. Sánchez writes that it is true that Marx once used the phrase "religion is the opium of the people," but that phrase does not transform Marxism into an antireligious movement. This phrase, he continues, which has so often been quoted, is unimportant and is taken from a seldom-read book Marx wrote before he worked out his philosophy of history. Sánchez also points out that there are many versions of the Marxist philosophy and even if some of them are antireligious, that does not prove that Marx's philosophy is the source of this antireligious feeling.[169]

The Apristas believe that the field of religion is different from that of politics. As Sánchez puts it, religion is the science of the absolute and politics is the art and science of the possible.[170] The Apristas say of themselves, therefore, "We are neither religious nor anti-religious: we are laymen."[171] Sánchez states that "Aprismo leaves to the conscience of each one of its members the resolving of the religious problem. Through experience it knows that mixing religion and politics kindles terrible fires."[172]

The Apristas see the purpose of their organization as the achievement of social justice through a struggle against imperialism and

[166] *Plan de acción*, p. 11.

[167] The Peruvian Constitution of 1933 reads as follows:

"Art. 232. Respecting the sentiments of the national majority, the State protects the Apostolic Roman Catholic Religion. Other religions enjoy freedom for the exercise of their respective faiths.

"Art. 233. The State exercises the national patronage in conformity with the laws and current practices."

[168] Luis Alberto Sánchez, *Aprismo y religión* (1933), p. 6.

[169] *Ibid.*, pp. 13–22.

[170] *Ibid.*, p. 11.

[171] *Ibid.*, p. 42.

[172] *Ibid.*, pp. 36–37.

against *"latifundismo criollo."* They do not think that religion should enter into this struggle which is economic, a class struggle between the oppressed and oppressing classes in Peru. Catholics, Protestants, atheists, and holders of other beliefs belong to the Peruvian Aprista party. All members are convinced that politics should be separated from religion. Sánchez writes that this conviction was based on the lesson given to Peru by President Leguía who, according to Sánchez, remained in power for eleven years with the complicity of the Church. Upon the fall of Leguía, many in Peru came to the conclusion that the connection between the Church and the State had been harmful to the Church. As a result, the national congress of the Peruvian Aprista party included in its program a demand for the separation of Church and State and the neutrality of the State in all religious questions.[173]

The leaders of the Aprista movement maintain this position, but claim that this does not make the movement antireligious. At times they criticize the Church for being a landlord and accuse it of fostering superstition among the Indians.[174] They advocate a state monopoly over education in order to destroy the Church's control, but the Apristas claim that recommending these changes has no relation to religion itself.[175] The Apristas say they are neutral in those matters which are purely religious. "The Catholic religion, just as all other religions, merits our equal respect. For Aprismo the horizons are political and consequently neither religious nor anti-religious: purely lay."[176] A pamphlet published by the Apristas states:

> The Peruvian Aprista Party is not a religious movement, but rather a social and political movement. Therefore, it never mixes into religious questions. It respects each person's religious ideas and proclaims that each person should be free to exercise his religious practices. Since the majority of the Peruvians are Apristas in politics and Catholics in religion, the Party democratically respects the sentiments and desires of its majority. Therefore, Aprismo frankly condemns all religious persecution.[177]

Seoane states that the Aprista movement purposely tries not to attack the Church in order to keep the social conflict based on economics. He claims that anticlericalism is an inheritance of the French revolution which, he thinks, should not become involved in the present social struggle. He claims that the religious feeling among the Peruvian people is, in large part, a result of their misery. He thinks that if the

[173] *Ibid.*, pp. 23–26.
[174] Seoane, *Nuestros fines*, pp. 32–33.
[175] Sánchez, *Aprismo y religión*, p. 29.
[176] *Ibid.*, p. 30; see also Haya de la Torre, *Política Aprista*, pp. 153–154.
[177] El Buró de Redactores de "Cuaderno Aprista," *40 preguntas y 40 respuestas*, p. 8.

Aprista movement could improve the economic lot of the people this would change their religious sentiments.[178]

If the Aprista movement is completely neutral in religious matters, why is it so determined to separate Church and State? Sánchez writes that "there is no tyranny no matter how bloody it may be, which does not protect the confessional schools and does not persecute the secular schools and secularism. For proof look at Venezuela, Cuba, Peru, Germany, Italy, Spain with Primo, Ecuador with García Moreno, Colombia with Reyes, Núñez, etc."[179]

Sánchez claims that the large landowners of Peru succeeded in having a part of the clergy attack the Peruvian Aprista party from the pulpit during election campaigns. He states that in Cuzco it was alleged that the Apristas were proposing the burning of churches, the violation of nuns, and the assassination of friars and believers.[180] Sánchez explains the opposition of the Church to the Aprista movement as follows:

> In Peru, as in the other countries of America, there is a high clergy and a low clergy. The high clergy is composed of the descendants of rich families which have donated their riches to the Church and received ecclesiastic positions (*prebendas*) for their relatives. This high clergy, oligarchical and allied to the *"civilista"* politicians, to whose class they belong, despises the lower national clergy. The separation is absolute. The lower national clergy, creole or Indian, feels itself displaced and, as happens in the game of partisan politics, replaced by the foreign clergy. They see this verified in an alliance, which is also economic, between the high clergy and the foreign clergy AGAINST THE LOW NATIONAL CLERGY (CREOLE OR INDIAN). This low clergy has a marked and logical sympathy for the Aprista movement while the high clergy and the foreign clergy (a sort of imperialism and latifundismo of the cassock) repudiate Aprismo. Just as the secular oligarchs and imperialists, those of the cassock, do not hesitate to utilize every kind of false charge against us.[181]

Three stories told by the Apristas seem to illustrate their true feelings about religion. Just before one of the Apristas was shot by a firing squad, he shouted to his wife, "Christ will save my soul and Apra will save Peru."[182] During the Trujillo revolt of 1932, when the Apristas held control of the city, they celebrated a mass.[183] Cossio del Pomar tells about an event which took place during the period when the Aprista movement was underground. One night Haya de la Torre was driving through the darkened streets of Lima, returning from a secret Aprista meeting, when he saw a priest walking. Stopping his auto, Haya picked

[178] Seoane, *Comunistas criollos,* pp. 35–38.
[179] Sánchez, *Aprismo y religión,* p. 31.
[180] *Ibid.,* p. 27.
[181] *Ibid.,* pp. 38–39. See also Partido Aprista Peruano, "El rol del alto clero," *El proceso Haya de la Torre,* pp. xxvi–xxviii.
[182] Sánchez, *Aprismo y religión,* p. 31.
[183] *Ibid.,* p. 30.

up the priest and drove him to his destination, which was the home of a dying person. As the priest got out of the car he asked Haya for his name so he could pray for him. Haya's answer was, "My name is not important. I am a good Christian who also travels at night doing something for the salvation of his fellow man. Pray for those who suffer persecution for the cause of justice." The priest left, saying, "God will pay you."[184]

Sánchez writes, "We are Catholic, but in a different sense, essentially we are agnostics. We are born in the Catholic faith and are loyal to it; but we are also imbued with a humanistic tradition, capable of understanding all faiths and of separating them from their political implications, which is not the case in some countries."[185]

The ideas about religion held by the Apristas can be summed up by saying that they want to relegate the Church to a position where it will not be involved in any activities which are not purely religious. For a country in which the Church has been established more than four hundred years, this is an exceedingly radical proposal and has not helped to make the Apristas popular with the Church.

[184] Cossio del Pomar, *Haya de la Torre, el indoamericano*, pp. 320–321.
[185] Luis Alberto Sánchez, "What's Left of Inter-Americanism," *Inter-American*, IV (Jan., 1945), 14.

CHAPTER V

THE APRISTAS AND THE SECOND WORLD WAR

EFFECT OF THE WAR UPON THE IDEAS OF THE APRISTA MOVEMENT

THE APRISTA ideology and program, discussed in the previous chapters, were affected by the Second World War, which caused the Apristas to modify their emphasis although they maintain that their basic ideas and program have not changed. The war led the Apristas to soften their criticism of and their opposition to United States imperialism. Until shortly before the beginning of the war the Apristas maintained that United States imperialism posed the greatest threat to Latin America because of is location and great power. With the approach of the war this emphasis changed. Nazism became the greatest threat, and fear of United States imperialism became subordinated. The war also led the Apristas to accentuate the democratic features of their program. They used the slogans emanating from the Western democracies as an additional argument for the establishment of democratic government in all Latin American countries where it was not present. At the same time, the Apristas claimed that the war emergency was another reason for adoption of their program which, they maintained, would enable Latin America to meet successfully the problems presented by the war.[1]

In the first years of the Aprista movement its leaders took a typically Marxian attitude toward war. They held that modern wars were a direct result of imperialistic rivalries. Since Latin America was not imperialistic, the Apristas claimed that it should not become involved in any such wars. The way for Latin America to prevent its involvement was to adopt the Aprista program, which would strengthen the area enough for it to hold itself aloof from war. As a result of this reasoning, the Aprista leaders predicted war long before the Second World War began. Haya de la Torre wrote in 1928 that war was inevitable as long as the system of economic and political relationships created by imperialism existed. Haya claimed that Latin America was one of the areas where the great powers fought each other economically and that

[1] The chief sources for the Aprista ideas on the war are: Manuel Seoane, *Nuestra América y la guerra* (1940); Víctor Raúl Haya de la Torre, *La defensa continental* (1942) and *Y después de la guerra ¿qué?* (1946).

it would inevitably become the scene of a new war unless it made itself strong enough to prevent that fate.[2]

Until about 1938 the Apristas continued to write in this manner. "Against War" was one of their oft-repeated slogans.[3] They continued to propose their maximum program as a means of avoiding involvement in a war. They claimed that if Latin America were united and strengthened by the expulsion of imperialism it would be strong enough to defend itself from any outside threat.

Two forces seem to have affected the Aprista viewpoint on war: the rise of the fascist powers and the Good Neighbor Policy of the United States. The Aprista leaders continued to argue that the war was caused by economic rivalry even after the beginning of military action in 1939. Nevertheless they decided that, in spite of the economic roots of the war, fascism presented a greater danger to Latin America than the economic imperialism of the United States and the Western allies.[4]

Before looking at the arguments presented by the Apristas against fascism, it is interesting to note the dates when they began to urge support of the Western democracies against the totalitarian powers. Haya de la Torre wrote an article in February, 1938, in which he warned of an approaching war.[5] At that time, he advocated coöperation between the United States and the Latin American republics in order to oppose the threat of international fascism. He suggested that this coöperation would be strengthened if democracy prevailed in all Latin America, and warned that United States imperialism would remain a threat even after the fascist powers were defeated. He ended by saying that the only road to Latin America's true salvation lay in the Aprista program: abolishing all imperialism in Latin America; economic and political unification of the area; and progressive nationalization of all its riches. These steps, he wrote, will assure the security and sovereignty of the people of Latin America on a basis of democracy and social justice.[6]

One of the Apristas, living in exile in Mexico, published a pamphlet in March, 1938, which attacked German, Italian, and Japanese penetration into Peru.[7] The pamphlet charged that these three countries were establishing bases in Peru for use in case of a war. The author claimed that the Italians were operating an airplane factory capable of

[2] Víctor Raúl Haya de la Torre, *El antimperialismo y el Apra* (1936), pp. 102–103.
[3] *Infra*, Appendix B, p. 134.
[4] Seoane, *op. cit.*, pp. 22–31.
[5] "El 'buen vecino:' ¿Garantía definitiva?," reprinted in *La defensa continental*, pp. 45–58.
[6] *Loc. cit.*
[7] Fernando León de Vivero, *Avance del imperialismo fascista en el Perú* (1938).

producing 250 to 300 airplanes a year when war began. He maintained that the port of Chicama was used as a base by German warships and submarines and that the Gildermeisters, a German family which owned a large sugar estate, were preparing to manufacture explosives out of sugar in case of war. He also charged that the Gildermeisters had erected a radio station on their estate which could reach Berlin and which was being used by the Germans for secret messages. The author of this pamphlet alleged that the Japanese colony in Peru could put 30,000 armed men into action at any time. According to the pamphlet, all three of these totalitarian groups coöperated with one another and all three had the support of the dictator of Peru, Benavides. The pamphlet also criticized Benavides for having brought into the country Italian military, aviation, and police missions which were introducing fascist methods within the armed forces. The pamphlet ends with the claim that the adoption of the Aprista program by Peru would enable it to end the fascist penetration of that country.[8]

Manuel Seoane issued a statement in behalf of the Aprista movement in March, 1939, when the war came closer.[9] He pointed out in this statement that the Axis powers were determined to conquer Latin America. He repeated the Aprista idea that the coming war was to be a struggle between two groups of imperialistic powers, but he insisted the United States was less of a danger to Latin America than the totalitarian powers. "The totalitarian danger," he wrote, "is the closest and most pressing."[10] Seoane did not see how an alliance of the twenty Latin American republics with the United States could do much good. It would be, he wrote, "the alliance of an elephant with twenty little cats."[11] Such an alliance, he thought, would not make the twenty-one nations allies, but rather would give the United States an additional burden. He proposed, therefore, that the Latin American republics should unite at once, both to be able to help the United States oppose fascism and to be able to oppose any future threat from the United States. Seoane ended his statement by writing: "In Indoamerica fascism shall not advance."[12]

When the war began, the Apristas continued to talk in this spirit. They wanted to see the fascist powers defeated, and they wanted the Latin American people to participate in that struggle so they would

[8] *Ibid., passim.*
[9] Reprinted in Seoane, *op. cit.,* pp. 176–183.
[10] *Ibid.,* p. 179.
[11] *Ibid.,* p. 180.
[12] *Ibid.,* p. 183.

have something to say about the peace that would be built after the war was over.[13]

The first authoritative statement by an Aprista leader to appear after the war began was Seoane's book *Nuestra América y la guerra.* He stated in the introduction that the book was being written in behalf of the Aprista movement and represented the collective thinking of its leaders.[14] The book urged the Latin American republics to help defeat the fascist powers by allying themselves with the United States and the Western European democracies.

Seoane claimed that the war had its roots in imperialistic rivalries and the hard peace created by the Treaty of Versailles. "The present war," he wrote, "just as almost all previous wars is a logical consequence of the system of capitalist rivalry."[15] This meant to Seoane that in addition to the ideological and psychological causes of the war the struggle for markets and raw materials caused by the capitalist organization of the contending powers was of great importance.[16] Despite this, Seoane believed that this war was different from previous wars in that it was a struggle between democratic imperialists and dictatorial imperialists. He did not think this difference altered the basic causes of the war, but believed it would greatly affect the results of the war. He advocated, therefore, that the Latin American republics coöperate with the United States and the Western European democracies to defeat the dictatorial powers.[17]

The main argument advanced by the Apristas for taking sides in the war was that it was a true world war, a universal struggle between the fascist and democratic forces in the world. The Apristas consider themselves the upholders of true democracy in Latin America—as soldiers in the war against dictatorship within Peru as well as within Latin America. When the war began, the Apristas said it was another phase of the world-wide struggle between democracy and dictatorship. The fact that the war was a struggle between two ideologically opposed groups made it different from the First World War. They claimed that in the new world war Latin America must support the democracies or the Nazis would crush it with the "brutal fanaticism of the Spaniards of the sixteenth century."[18]

[13] Haya de la Torre, *Y después de la guerra ¿qué?*, pp. 22–27.
[14] Seoane, *op. cit.*, p. 15.
[15] *Ibid.*, p. 24.
[16] *Ibid.*, p. 31.
[17] *Ibid.*, *passim.*
[18] Víctor Raúl Haya de la Torre, "Latin America Fears Invasion," *Living Age*, vol. 359 (Oct., 1940), 146–147; Alfredo Saco, "El arsenal de la América Latina," *Norte, revista continental,* vol. 2 (March, 1942), 5–7.

Haya de la Torre expounded the Aprista viewpoint on the war in his book *La defensa continental.* He pointed out that certain groups in Latin America claimed that the war did not really concern Latin America; that it was a war between two imperialistic blocs and, therefore, neutrality was the best policy for Latin America since the contenders in the war were both dangerous to it. Haya's answer to this contention was that neutrality would be sensible only if the war were purely economic. He claimed that this was not true, but rather that this war had political and ideological sources more important than the economic causes of the war. The ideology of Nazism is racist, said Haya, and this racism makes it a greater threat to Latin America than the purely economic imperialism of its opponents.

Nazism is the great threat to Latin America, Haya continued, because it maintains that men are inferior or superior according to the blood in their veins and the color of their skins. Latin America must fear the victory of Nazism, for its victory would bring not only economic hegemony for Germany but the racial subjugation of all non-Aryans.[19] Haya admitted that economic imperialism was bad, but claimed that where it was present a worker could sometimes improve his status if fate permitted. On the other hand, he said, "He who is born black or an Indian, a quadroon or a mestizo, cannot modify the color of his skin or willingly modify the facial angles. As one is born, one remains, a white aryan, a Negro, yellow, red, or mestizo."[20] Latin Americans, therefore, must be opposed to Nazi fascism. Capitalism is bad, Haya continued, but racism is worse. In *Mein Kampf* Hitler clearly stated what he thought of the people of Latin America: they were an inferior race. Haya then asked the question: "If the European Jews—so many of them so blond and fair—have been persecuted and oppressed because their race is not pure, what are we able to expect for the Indians and mestizos who constitute eighty-five per cent of this vast continent we inhabit?"[21]

Haya pointed out another advantage to Latin America in favoring the capitalist, imperialistic countries over the Axis. This advantage originated in the fact that democracy exists in the great capitalist countries, Britain and the United States. Democracy existed there before capitalism did as evidence by the fact that the Magna Carta, Cromwell's revolution, and the United States Bill of Rights all preceded

---

[19] Haya de la Torre, *La defensa continental,* pp. 97–98; Seoane uses the same argument in *Nuestra América y la guerra,* pp. 108–109.
[20] Haya de la Torre, *La defensa continental,* p. 99.
[21] *Ibid.,* pp. 100–101.

financial industrialism. Liberty to struggle against evil remains in the democratic countries. It does not remain in the totalitarian countries. For Haya the conclusion was clear: the democratic organization of the capitalist countries leaves open the road to progress. This is the key difference, he maintained, between being pro-Nazi and being in favor of the democracies and, therefore, Latin Americans could not be neutral.[22] Haya summed up this aspect of the Aprista point of view by saying:

> We are always anti-imperialists, but we are always democrats. We struggle for the abolition of all imperialism no matter whether it comes from totalitarian countries or from where democracy exists. Yet we reject and we combat totalitarianism which wishes to replace the inhuman differences of economic imperialism with other differences of race.
>
> Our position in this struggle is to defend democracy and its essence, liberty. And to use liberty to abolish imperialism and to try by means of what is called "Dynamic Democracy" (I as an Aprista say functional democracy) to conquer political equality and perfecting that to open the roads to economic justice among men and among nations.[23]

Seoane could also see differences between the imperialism emanating from the two contending blocks in the war. He pointed out that the imperialism of the United States and Great Britain was financial; it resulted in capital coming to Latin America. He contrasted this to Japanese imperialism which usually penetrated a Latin American country by sending a mass of colonists who used Japanese funds to take over all the small businesses in an area. Seoane stated that German penetration into a country also was based on concentrated colonies which continued to use the German language and created the problem of the foreign minority. Seoane's conclusion was that a victory for the United States and Britain would be more advantageous to Latin America than a victory for Germany and Japan.[24]

Seoane pointed out another reason why Latin America should participate in the war: it was impossible for her to remain neutral. "Indoamerica," he wrote, "is condemned sooner or later to play the same role as Belgium and Holland; that is, it will be a battlefield in the tremendous conflict between the two groups of powers who are contesting for the rule of the world."[25] He came to this conclusion because he predicted that the United States would inevitably enter the war. (Seoane was writing in 1940.) On the day that occurred, he predicted, the Latin

[22] *Ibid.*, pp. 101–103.
[23] *Ibid.*, pp. 103–104.
[24] Seoane, *op. cit.*, pp. 113–115.
[25] *Ibid.*, p. 47.

American republics would be at war whether they wanted to be or not. Latin America, he wrote, is a natural base for an attack upon the Panama Canal. The United States will try to prevent its use for this purpose by the Nazis, and the Nazis will try to utilize it for this purpose. No matter which is successful, Seoane concluded, Latin America will not be able to remain neutral even if it tries to do so.[26]

Another reason Seoane thought Latin America could not stay out of the war was that it was both rich in raw materials and weak in military resources. This put Latin America in danger, because since the war was basically an economic war Latin America would be part of the booty of that war. To support this reasoning Seoane pointed to Hitler's statements about Latin America and the activity of the Nazi groups. These all demonstrated, to Seoane, that the Nazis intended to conquer Latin America.[27]

The Aprista movement was illegal in Peru during the war, hence it was unable to demonstrate its sincerity by doing anything concrete about fighting fascism. It did, however, advocate active intervention in the war by the Latin American republics,[28] and proposed that the United Nations create a Latin American division of volunteers to fight under its command alongside the armed forces of the democratic powers. This was suggested, the Apristas said, because the dictatorial governments of many Latin American countries gave only oral support to the fight against the totalitarian powers. The dictator of Peru refused to send the Peruvian army against the Nazis. Other Latin American countries also refused to send their armies against the Nazis; therefore, the Apristas believed, an inter-American army should be organized which could enter the fight despite the failure of certain governments to take action.[29]

Although the Apristas labeled the Nazis as the main enemy of the Latin American people, they insisted that, despite their critics, they had not changed their opinion of United States imperialism.[30] They

---

[26] *Ibid.*, pp. 32–47.

[27] *Ibid.*, pp. 63–97.

[28] Haya de la Torre, *Y después de la guerra ¿qué?*, p. 22.

[29] *Ibid.*, pp. 25–26; Víctor Raúl Haya de la Torre, Letter to the Editor, New York *Times*, Dec. 25, 1942, p. 16.

[30] What the Apristas objected to were statements similar to the following by Professor Whitaker: "At least a year before the break between Germany and Russia, the leaders of the corresponding radical group in Peru, the APRA had already begun to recant their former Yankeephobia and to call on liberals and radicals in Latin America to co-operate with the United States in the defense of democracy against totalitarianism. This was the theme of public declarations made as early as 1940 by two of the leading Apristas, Manuel Seoane and Luis Alberto Sánchez, and in the summer of 1941 it was incorporated in the official doctrine of the party by the

claimed that the change that occurred was in United States policy. The Democratic "good neighbor" had taken the place of the Republican "big stick." In fact, Haya de la Torre said, the Latin American anti-imperialist attitude had a great influence on the change in attitude by the United States. This was especially true of the activity of Sandino and the policy followed by certain countries, particularly Mexico, Argentina, Bolivia, and Chile. The Apristas, said Haya, have looked with sympathy at the change in United States policy which has improved inter-American relations.[31] As Luis Alberto Sánchez put it: "If the 'Good Neighbor Policy' has improved relations between the two Americas, it is because former relations were not so good; if one grants that relations were good, there would be no reason to applaud the 'Good Neighbor Policy' as an encouraging and decisive occurrence."[32]

Several leaders of the Aprista movement visited the United States during the war, and this may have helped them to arrive at a better understanding of its people and the policies of its government. Both Manuel Seoane and Luis Alberto Sánchez wrote sympathetic accounts of their trips, which received wide circulation in Latin America.[33] Alfredo Saco, another Aprista leader, worked in the Washington Office of the Coördinator of Inter-American Affairs. Despite the more intimate knowledge acquired by these visits, the Apristas continued to see Latin America threatened by the United States. Sánchez wrote that he observed a superiority complex in many of the people of the United States. He thought this feeling of superiority combined with the tremendous military power which the United States would wield after the war might make it a danger to its neighbors. He wrote that the military victory of either the United States or the totalitarian powers was to be feared, and he qualified this by saying the United States victory would be a lesser evil.[34]

The war strengthened the conviction held by the Apristas that its program for Latin America was essentially correct. They argued: "Only

---

supreme leader, Víctor Raúl Haya de la Torre, who made it the main theme of a new program for the APRA." Arthur P. Whitaker, "Politics and Diplomacy in 1941," *Inter-American Affairs—1941* (1942), p. 46. In a letter to the editor of the *Diario de Costa Rica*, Haya de la Torre said on this subject, "I am not able to affirm that I have been converted into a friend of the United States from being a foe of the United States. I have never been a foe of the United States but of United States economic imperialism." Reprinted in *La defensa continental*, p. 135.

[31] Haya de la Torre, *La defensa continental*, pp. 135–137.

[32] Luis Alberto Sánchez, "A New Interpretation of the History of America," *Hispanic American Historical Review*, XXIII (August, 1943), 453.

[33] Manuel Seoane, *El gran vecino* (1942); Luis Alberto Sánchez, *Un sudamericano en Norteamérica* (1942).

[34] Sánchez, *Un sudamericano en Norteamérica*, pp. 371–377.

in the five-point maximum program of the Aprista doctrine will the Indoamerican peoples find their defense and the road to liberation."[35] This was a constant note in the Aprista writings. To them, their program would solve everything that needed solving in Latin America, or at least put Latin America upon a road which would lead to the solution of its problems. That is why they continued to urge the adoption of their five-point program. Now is the time, said Haya de la Torre, to inter-Americanize the Panama Canal, for if all of us should defend it all of us should own it. Inter-Americanization of the canal, he wrote, would not only be of economic benefit to Latin America in cheaper tolls, but it would be a firm pledge given by the United States that imperialism would not reappear in the relations between the two Americas.[36]

The Apristas believed that the war made unification of Latin America more imperative than ever. Seoane claimed that only unification could strengthen the area enough for it to play a role in the war. He thought even unification would not prevent Hitler's armies from conquering the area unless the United States aided in its defense, but he did think that unification would result in more strength to defend the area.[37] Another advantage that would result from unification, according to Seoane, was that Latin America would be able to make its voice heard at the peace table when the war was over. He predicted that the voice of the small country would be ignored when the peace was written, whereas a unified Latin America would have to be heard. Seoane proposed that since it seemed impossible to unite all of Latin America at the moment a beginning should be made by creating five countries to take the place of the twenty republics. He advocated a reorganization along these lines: (*a*) the Confederation of North and Central America to include Mexico, Guatemala, El Salvador, Costa Rica, Nicaragua, and Honduras; (*b*) the Confederation of the Caribbean to include Venezuela, Colombia, Cuba, the Dominican Republic, Panama, and Haiti; (*c*) the Confederation of Brazil; (*d*) the Confederation of the Plata River to include Argentina, Uruguay, and Paraguay; and (*e*) the Confederation of the Pacific to include Ecuador, Peru, Chile, and Bolivia. Seoane believed that only the first step would be difficult. He pointed out that the thirteen English colonies became the great United States once they had taken the first step. He claimed that if the twenty Latin American republics take the first steps toward union the inter-American confederation would develop.[38]

---

[35] León de Vivero, *op. cit.*, p. 38; El Buró de Redactores de "Cuaderno Aprista," *40 preguntas y 40 respuestas, sobre el Partido Aprista Peruano* (1941), pp. 12–14.
[36] Haya de la Torre, *La defensa continental,* pp. 137–138.
[37] Seoane, *Nuestra América y la guerra,* pp. 117–131.
[38] Seoane, *El gran vecino,* pp. 327–330.

The Apristas utilized the war for a campaign to introduce more democracy into Latin America. Their argument was that if the war was against tyranny and dictatorship it should be a fight against all tyrants instead of against only certain dictators.[39] Haya de la Torre pointed out that it was difficult for many Latin Americans to get excited about a war for democracy in Europe or Asia when they, themselves, lived where there was none. "If the World War," he said, "has as its aim the victory of democracy against dictatorship, here in Latin America dictatorships exist which must be conquered that democracy may triumph."[40] The Apristas maintained that to create a real inter-American front against fascist penetration it was necessary to have democracy introduced into those countries of Latin America where it did not exist. Haya stressed the fact that only the people who felt the benefits of democracy could really fight to preserve it. On the other hand, he wrote, when a Latin American dictatorship declared war on Germany and issued statements about democracy, the people living in a country of this type were not impressed.[41]

When the Havana Conference of the Foreign Ministers of the American Republics voted a resolution to fight the fifth column in Latin America, Haya de la Torre raised the question, "What if the governments themselves are the fifth column?"[42] He answered by saying the governments of many of the Latin American states were fifth columns, if by that term were meant people who worked for totalitarianism and against democracy. He claimed that a government that talked about democracy and abolished all freedom for its people was a fifth column against democracy.[43]

Haya declared that a fifth column was a modern name for organized treason, but that the Trojan horse was not the true symbol for the fifth column. Rather, he suggested, the prototypes were Judas, the initiator of the fifth column in the ranks of Christianity, and the Indian renegade, Felipillo, who helped Pizarro capture Atahualpa and conquer the Inca Empire. Felipillo, Haya said, was the precursor of the fifth columns at the service of the enemies of the liberty of the American people. The German, Italian, and Japanese fifth columns would not be difficult to handle; the difficult thing, he argued, is to handle the Felipillos who are part of a country and yet conspire against it. These

---

[39] Seoane, *Nuestra América y la guerra*, p. 144.

[40] Víctor Raúl Haya de la Torre, "Toward a Real Inter-Americanism," *Free World*, vol. 3 (July, 1942), 163–164.

[41] *Loc. cit.*

[42] Haya de la Torre, *La defensa continental*, p. 143.

[43] *Loc. cit.*

enemies of the people, in many cases, are the dictatorial governments themselves, which are the best fifth columns totalitarianism could want.[44]

Haya de la Torre's complaint was that the Havana Conference and President Roosevelt talked about the danger of the fifth column in Latin America but failed to recognize that certain governments were themselves acting as a fifth column by fighting democracy within their own country. Haya claimed that the Latin American supporters of democracy were not impressed when they saw the resolution against the fifth column presented to the Havana Conference by the Brazilian delegation, which represented the dictatorial government of Getulio Vargas. Haya wondered whether President Roosevelt knew there were differences between his government and the dictatorships of Latin America.[45] He pointed out that the leaders of the United States talked about the people oppressed by dictators in Europe, while the United States government treated as equals the tyrannies of Guatemala and Peru and the democracies of Colombia, Costa Rica, and Chile.[46]

The Apristas also claimed that the undemocratic governments in Latin America were being strengthened during the war by the support they received from other countries, particularly the United States. Sánchez charged that "by and large, United States lend-lease aid to Latin America has gone to the dictators." He concluded: "In Latin America, the war has further impoverished the poor and enriched the wealthy. It has increased the army's power, both politically and militarily."[47]

Taking this into account, the Apristas claim that there is no such thing as nonintervention and that the United States policy of nonintervention has the effect of helping to strengthen undemocratic governments in Latin America. The Apristas come to this conclusion, they say, because the recognition of an illegal government, the advancing of

[44] *Ibid.*, pp. 141–142; Manuel Seoane charged that the dictatorial government of Peru coöperated with the Japanese elements in Peru. "The Peruvian constitution states that Mayors are to be elected by the people. But for the past quarter century this custom has occasionally been ignored. Strong Peruvian governments, afraid that an Aprista might be elected, have directly appointed the Mayors. Thus Okada (a Japanese) was appointed Mayor of Huaral and several other Japanese held the post in Virú, Maldonado, and Ayacucho, three important cities of the 'hinterland.' Therefore, it was better to be a Japanese than an Aprista in Peru. I myself, for example, am the son, grandson, and great-grandson of Peruvians, on both my mother's and father's side yet I have never been able to reach Okada's position of power, although I was elected a Deputy of the Chamber in Lima by 30,000 votes." "The Japanese are Still in Peru," *Asia and the Americas*, vol. 43 (Dec., 1943), 675.

[45] Haya de la Torre, *La defensa continental*, pp. 141–145.

[46] *Ibid.*, pp. 188–189.

[47] Luis Alberto Sánchez, "What's Left of Inter-Americanism," *Inter-American*, IV (March, 1945), 13.

loans to it, and other relations with it are a form of intervention that helps the dictatorial regimes to stay in power by cloaking them with an aura of respectability.[48]

The Apristas think the democratic governments of the world, and especially the government of the United States, should look to the Latin American democrats for friendship.[49] The Apristas, as a matter of course, regard their movement as the type of organization the United States should encourage and claim this has never been done.[50] When the war ended, Seoane stated that the United States policy of giving "economic aid to Latin America served to keep the dictators in power, causing the nations to believe that the Great Neighbor was willing to scorn their rightful democratic hopes for the sake of supporting the tyrants." He wrote further: "The Good Neighbor Policy is a doctrine of 'good manners.' But we want one of good aims as well."[51]

Plan for the Affirmation of Democracy in Latin America

At the beginning of the war, Haya de la Torre proposed a "Plan for the affirmation of democracy in America," which, he claimed, would help both to strengthen Latin American democracy and to defeat the totalitarian powers.[52] The plan was approved by the Peruvian Aprista party in 1941 and received much publicity in Latin America. The plan combined ideas from the Aprista maximum program with ideas from the Aprista program for Peru and used the war as a compelling reason for its adoption. The plan was based on the proposition that all the people of America aspired to see democracy in America. The Apristas believed that the plan would help to achieve democracy because it would affirm it in its political, juridical, and economic aspects.

The Aprista plan stated that the world was faced with a choice between democracy and totalitarianism. It defined democracy as a system based on popular sovereignty as the base of the national sovereignty of the state. Totalitarianism was defined as a system where the dictator-

[48] Manuel Seoane, "The South American Trojan Horse," *The Nation*, vol. 155 (Nov. 14, 1942), 508.

[49] *Ibid.*, pp. 508–509.

[50] Hubert Herring, writing in 1941, reported that "our embassy in Lima never admits by word or deed that they have ever heard of the Apristas. In January, 1941, Haya de la Torre sent a representative to the embassy with a message of congratulations for President Roosevelt upon his third inauguration. The envoy was not admitted, the message was not accepted for transmission. Ambassador Norweb was meticulously correct." *Good Neighbors* (1941), p. 348.

[51] Manuel Seoane, "Where Do We Go From Here?," *Inter-American*, V (March, 1946), 23.

[52] The plan is reprinted in *La defensa continental*, pp. 216–234 and in *Almanaque la tribuna 1948*, pp. 228–234.

ship is sovereign. Democracy, the plan declared, establishes a balance between the liberty of the citizen, limited by that of his fellow citizens, and the liberty of the state, limited by that of other states. Totalitarianism eradicates this equilibrium by abolishing the liberty of its citizens and of other states to create the supreme liberty of the totalitarian state. Another difference between democracy and totalitarianism, outlined by the plan, was that in a democracy force was at the service of the law, whereas in a totalitarian state force became the only law.[53]

The plan claimed that all the countries of America were agreed that it should be defended from the totalitarian danger. Indoamerica was particularly aware of the need for defense because the racial doctrines of the Nazis posed a special threat to the varied peoples who inhabited the area. The fact that one of the twenty-one American states was so much more powerful than the other twenty presented certain problems, yet both the one powerful state and the twenty weak states were agreed that there should be a united defense against the threat from Europe.[54]

Both the United States and Latin America, the plan continued, face the problem of improving their democracy. The United States system of capitalist production creates a problem of internal economic and social inequality and threatens Latin America with its imperialistic expansion. The Latin American dictatorships and oligarchies are an obstacle to democracy and many times have been rescued and strengthened by United States capitalist expansion.[55]

The plan then claimed that the totalitarian threat could be defeated only when democracy had been so strengthened that it became a living force upheld by the faith of people. Democracy, the plan maintained, is the same everywhere. Its fundamental feature is liberty for the citizen combined with the existence of freely elected governments subject to fixed legal rights and duties. Since democracy is indivisible, according to the plan, it must be defended by all twenty-one countries when it is in danger in any one of them.[56]

After the long introduction, the "Plan for the affirmation of democracy in America" made two proposals, one political and one economic. The political proposal was that an inter-American congress meet to declare that the democratic liberties listed in the twenty-one constitutions of the American republics were the base of the continent's democratic sovereignty. The inter-American congress would combine the

[53] Haya de la Torre, *La defensa continental*, pp. 217–218.
[54] *Ibid.*, pp. 218–220.
[55] *Ibid.*, pp. 220–221.
[56] *Ibid.*, pp. 221–225.

provisions dealing with democracy listed in each of the twenty-one constitutions into one document which would be the basis of an inter-American treaty. The treaty would declare that when any of these principles are not honored in any of the twenty-one states the other twenty states have the right to demand they be honored in order to protect democracy in the hemisphere. The document listing the democratic rights for all Americans would be called the Magna Carta of America. It would perpetuate the interdependent principles of popular sovereignty, national sovereignty, and continental sovereignty.[57]

Under the proposed treaty the people of any American state would be able to demand the aid of the other states when its government violated democratic liberties. This, according to the Aprista plan, would be an extension of the principle adopted at the Havana meeting of the foreign ministers of the American republics. There it was decided that any American state could demand aid of the other states when its democratic stability was threatened by the work of a foreign fifth column.[58]

A permanent inter-American organ would be created to carry out the work envisioned by the Aprista plan. It would be a judicial body or arbitral tribunal which would settle disputes which arose about the interpretations of a constitutional provision dealing with democratic liberties. This permanent organ for all America would have permanent subcommittees in each of the twenty-one republics. The subcommittees would be composed of representatives of the executive, legislative, and judicial powers of the country, of representatives of all large, democratic political parties, of the universities, and of the inter-American body.[59]

What the plan proposed was a method of collective intervention to preserve democracy. Haya de la Torre claimed that the creation of a system of this kind would not only defend democracy, but prevent aggression in America. Aggression, he claimed further, always began with the subjection of the people in the home country and then proceeded against other countries. He maintained that the war against Germany was a collective intervention to prevent Germany from conquering the world. He also compared the work of the proposed international organ to the work of a police force. The police, he wrote, act against individuals only when they transgress the law. In the same way, collective intervention would act against undemocratic govern-

[57] *Ibid.*, pp. 225–226.
[58] *Ibid.*, pp. 226–227.
[59] *Ibid.*, pp. 227–228.

ments only when they transgressed the "common law" of America.[60] Seoane wrote that this proposed court would be "a collective judge embodying the plural democratic will of the continent."[61]

The proposal for collective intervention to protect democratic liberties in America received much publicity in 1945 when the Uruguayan foreign minister, Eduardo Rodríguez Larreta, proposed such action. No concrete result came from his proposal. The Bogotá Conference of the American states in 1948, however, discussed this subject and adopted a resolution asking the Inter-American Juridical Committee to study the question and to prepare a draft statute on the subject of creating an Inter-American court to protect the rights of man.[62]

The economic section of the Aprista plan is a projection to the continental scene of the idea of having a national economic congress plan Peru's development. The proposal is that an economic congress meet in each of the twenty-one republics. These congresses would be made up of the representatives of all the vital forces of each country's production, distribution, and consumption: capital, labor, industry, agriculture, and commerce, including foreign interests in the case of the Latin American countries. These congresses would study each country's economy and formulate a plan for the internal economic development within each state. Each economic congress would create a permanent consultative council which would have the task of advising the government of each country on how to develop the economy. The national councils would also foster regional meetings.

After the twenty-one national economic congresses and the regional congresses completed their work, an inter-American economic congress would meet to coördinate the proposals made by the national congresses and work out an inter-American economic plan. The Aprista plan suggested the following as necessary reforms which the economic congress should approve:

1. The creation of an Indoamerican monetary unit based on gold, silver, and raw materials which would be stable in relation to the dollar.

---

[60] Víctor Raúl Haya de la Torre, quoted in *Peruvian Times*, July 6, 1945, pp. 2, 20.

[61] Seoane, "Where Do We Go From Here?," *Inter-American*, V (March, 1946), 25.

[62] See Arthur P. Whitaker, "Inter-American Intervention," *Current History*, vol. 10 (March, 1946), 206–211; Ricardo J. Alfaro, "La intervención colectiva de la republicas americanas," *Revista de derecho internacional* (Habana), XLVIII (Dec., 1945), 153–162; the Bogotá resolution is number XXXI in United States. Department of State, *Ninth International Conference of American States, Bogotá, Colombia, March 30–May 2, 1948, Report of the Delegation of the United States of America with Related Documents* (1948), p. 266; this subject is also discussed in Inter-American Emergency Advisory Committee for Political Defense, Third Annual Report, First Section, *A Study of Conditions Necessary to Assure Political Defense* (1947).

2. The creation of an inter-American bank with branches in each country to stimulate commerce and productive investments.

3. The establishment of an inter-American customs union.

4. The stimulation of and the lowering of the cost of transportation and the means of communication.

5. The equalization of transit fees through the Panama Canal for all American states.

6. The creation of a body to make a study of the following: cöoperatives, methods of protecting workers and improving their conditions, techniques of improving agriculture, ways of increasing the continent's capacity to absorb continental products.

The economic congress would also propose measures to prevent the capital invested in each state from becoming an instrument of exploitation or oppression.[63]

The Aprista plan then suggested that Pan Americanism be replaced with a new concept of coöperation and justice which would lead to a united America, since "Inter-American relations have to equate the importance of the national sovereignty of the states with the popular sovereignty of their citizens. From this equilibrium can emerge the continental sovereignty of the Americas whose *raison d'être* is political and economic democracy."[64]

The plan ends by stating that when true democratic liberties are exercised and protected in each country and in inter-American relations then both the people and the states of this hemisphere would be able to live without fear. This, the plan claimed, would be democratic inter-Americanism without empire.[65]

The Aprista "Plan for the affirmation of democracy in America" never was put into practice, but its provisions help one to understand the Aprista ideology. It is doubtful whether the basic premise of the plan—that all of the people of America aspired to see democracy instituted in the continent—could have been true. The fact that there is so little democracy demonstrates that there are people who do not want it or who are unaware of its need.

A review of the effect of the last war upon the ideas and program advocated by the Apristas demonstrates that they were not basically changed during the course of the war. Whatever changes occurred were in emphasis rather than in principle. The Apristas were true to their democratic philosophy and opposed the totalitarian powers; they con-

[63] Haya de la Torre, *La defensa continental,* pp. 228–233; see also pp. 172–182.
[64] *Ibid.,* p. 234.
[65] *Loc. cit.*

tinued to point to the Aprista maximum program as the solution for all of Latin America's problems; they tried to use the war as a means of instituting democracy in the republics of Latin America where it did not exist, particularly Peru; and they applauded the Good Neighbor Policy of the United States while they continued to warn of the dangers of United States imperialism.

Haya de la Torre summed up the Aprista point of view very well in 1944. "Aprismo," he said, "continues in its course. It is against Nazi-fascism because that presents the greatest imperialist danger, since it is economic, political, and racist imperialism all at the same time. But Aprismo is against all imperialism always, even when it comes from democratic nations. Aprismo is for the union of the Indoamerican peoples, for only then will they be strong, forming a true 'continental people' in this age in which only states of this type are ranked as great powers. Aprismo is for democracy and social justice as the inseparable benefits of a confederated or amphictyonic Indoamerican organization. And Aprismo is for living together with the United States of Northamerica on the basis of democratic inter-Americanism without empire."[66]

[66] Haya de la Torre, *Y después de la guerra ¿qué?*, p. 239.

CHAPTER VI

APRISMO: AN EVALUATION

MODERN WORLD politics is dominated at this time by the political theories of the two major world powers. The spokesmen for the private capitalist democracy of the United States maintain that it exemplifies all that is valuable in the heritage of Western civilization. The theorists of the Soviet Union claim that the present structure of society in their country is a model which all countries eventually will imitate. Offering an alternative to the two major political theories are the movements and organizations which have been called a "third force" in world politics. The advocates of the "third force" visualize a world which has abandoned both private capitalism and Soviet totalitarianism in favor of an organization of society containing the good from both without their evils. Organizations prominent within the "third force" are the Socialist parties of France, India, and the United States; the labor parties of Great Britain, Scandinavia, Australia, and New Zealand; and the Co-operative Commonwealth Federation of Canada.

Democratic socialism is the term that best describes the aims of the organizations in the "third force." The Aprista thinkers belong to this school of political theory because they accept its most important features: its accent upon democracy and its insistence that the state has a right—and the duty—to place social need above any individual claim. They advocate, therefore, state intervention in the reconstruction of social and economic institutions in order to satisfy the social needs of its citizens.

A thorough study of the ideology and program of the Aprista movement suggests that it is not a completely new political thought. The Aprista leaders, however, have combined certain ideas about the unique character of Latin America with the general ideas of democratic socialism in such a way that they comprise a doctrine which is a distinctive contribution to the political theory of Latin America. It is original only in that it is different from all other proposed solutions of the problems of the area. The Aprista ideology has its weaknesses, the most conspicuous being its neglect of a method of achieving power, but it is an impressive attempt to create a political program suitable to Latin American conditions.

The Aprista doctrine proposes many changes in the organization of life in an area where powerful forces strive to preserve the status quo.

As a result, the Aprista proposals become revolutionary—although similar programs are accepted or advocated in the United States and other democracies without arousing violent opposition and sometimes without arousing any great interest. Universal education, democracy, adequate taxation, state intervention into economic life, and the other Aprista proposals are not considered revolutionary in the democratic countries. Even the proposal for the unification of the twenty Latin American republics is not very revolutionary when compared with the aims of organizations such as the World Federalists. Peru's comparative backwardness, however, makes the Aprista ideas revolutionary, for their introduction would transform life in that country.

It is possible that the leaders of the Aprista movement are utopians for believing that Peru can be transformed into a modern, democratic state after it has existed without democracy for so long a time, yet this is what they attempt to do. The Apristas advocate a program which they believe will create a democratic Peru, one which allows its people a chance to gain a decent livelihood, is progressive in education and industrialization, and is part of a democratic federation of Latin American states. Whether this program should be adopted by the people of Peru and Latin America can be answered only on the basis of a critic's predilection, but those who believe in democracy should sympathize with the Aprista aims.

A thorough study suggests that the refusal of the Peruvian ruling class to tolerate any efforts at reform may have been responsible for the development of the Aprista movement in Peru. A group of brilliant young students organized in an attempt to reform the University of San Marcos in Lima and were eventually pushed into politics. Radical student movements developed in other Latin American countries after the First World War, but it was only in Peru that the student organization was transformed into a political movement.

The new information which became available in the early 1920's about the antiquity of the Indian civilizations of Peru, together with the teachings of González Prada and Mariátegui, stimulated the interest of the Lima students in the conditions of the Peruvian Indians. It must be remembered that many of the students who were to be the future leaders of the Aprista movement were born in Trujillo, Cuzco, and other provincial cities where the ruins of ancient civilizations were an everyday sight. As a result of this interest in the Indians, the first important project undertaken by the students was the creation of night schools in order to raise the educational, economic, and social level of the illiterate—and in this way recapture the heritage of the past. The administration of President Leguía stifled this effort by closing the Universidades Popular González Parada, as the night schools had been named. It is possible that this was the decisive point in the evolution of the students' thinking; if the Peruvian government had not opposed their effort to educate the illiterate, the Aprista movement might never have developed.

The Leguía administration did more than close the adult education centers. It imprisoned and exiled many of the student leaders. Thus a group of energetic young men and women found themselves either in jail, where they had much time to think, or in exile, where they could gather fresh impressions. The actions of the Peruvian government also appear to have convinced the young students that political activity was essential to enable them to achieve their aims of educating the underprivileged.

Convinced of the need for political action, the young Peruvian exiles traveled during a period which taught them much about politics. They observed the Mexican revolutionary scene, the turmoil of the early days of the Bolshevik revolution in Russia, the rise of fascism in Germany and Italy, the general strike in Britain, and other stimulating events. They lived in Argentina, Chile, Ecuador, Mexico, and other American countries, and in Europe. Probably because they were an unusually gifted group, they used their time in exile to study the political and economic organization of the countries they visited. While in exile, they founded the Aprista organization. The first political campaign by the Peruvian Aprista party took place in the elections of 1931. The attempt by the dictatorship of Sánchez Cerro to destroy the new party tended to temper it, and the fourteen years of underground activity that followed molded the Aprista movement as free activity might not have done.

The Aprista thinkers have made their chief contribution in their far-reaching suggestions about the future organization of Latin America. They visualize a reorganized continent which has assimilated its Indian population. They see the continent industrialized and democratized. It would be a powerful, unified nation-state, inhabited by a healthy, educated, progressive people, which would play an important role in world affairs. The language of the Aprista leaders in describing the Latin America they visualize is at times bombastic and florid, but the picture they paint is an attractive one for all who believe in democracy, equality, and progress. Although the specific proposals made by the Aprista thinkers to implement their broad plans are sometimes utopian, the general conception is one of a better life for all Latin Americans. Those who accept the assumption made by the Apristas—that all men and women are entitled to a share in the economic and political control of their destinies—are forced to conclude that the Aprista movement is only an expression of the everlasting yearning by the masses for a better life.

The Apristas devote much effort to arguing that Latin America is different from Europe and the United States, hence must cease imitating their economic and political institutions. They argue that Latin America is unique because it is the home of two opposing cultures, one derived from Europe and the other derived from its indigenous population. Although the Europeans were able to conquer the area and institute their economic system, they were never able to exterminate or assimilate the Indians. Millions of Indians continue to live as their ancestors did. History demonstrates, however, that a stable society is possible only where a people are in agreement about the basic rules to be used in the conduct of affairs. Because agreement does not exist—as Professor Tannenbaum points out—"no national culture can be built and no political stability can be had without some means of encompassing the total population of Peru, Guatemala, Bolivia, and Ecuador within the framework of what is now the state."[1] The Aprista thinkers agree with this viewpoint and argue that it applies to all Latin America. They believe that their program would amalgamate the Indian and Europeanized sections of the population and produce a new integrated Indoamerican culture which would contain elements taken from both. It is impossible to demonstrate that the Aprista program would accomplish this aim, but the Apristas appear to be stressing a valid point.

As a result of their insistence upon the unique character of Latin America, the Apristas claim to repudiate "foreign" ideas. In developing their program, however, they took many ideas from their study and observation of foreign lands. They maintain this is not a contradiction, because what they have adopted is capable of being integrated into the Latin American social scene. They repudiate foreign ideas not because they are foreign, but because in many cases the attempt is made to introduce copied ideas and methods without trying to fit them into the rhythm of Latin American life. The Apristas emphasize that the Spanish government kept firm control of its colonies and as a result the ruling group in Latin America looked overseas for assistance and leadership.

[1] Frank Tannenbaum, "Agrarismo, indianismo, y nacionalismo," *Hispanic American Historical Review*, XXIII (August, 1943), 422.

Because Latin America has remained a colony economically, the Apristas argue that its ruling groups have developed an intellectual colonialism which keeps them looking abroad for their ideas.

It would appear obvious that political thought should be based upon the conditions of life in an area, but this has not been the case in Latin America. Professor Arthur P. Whitaker points out, "The continuity of foreign influence upon political thought in Latin America should be stressed, for it is too often forgotten or ignored."[2] There is much evidence, however, that Latin American imitation of other areas is not as prevalent as it was in the past. Professor Federico G. Gil thinks that "Latin America as a whole is groping toward a more realistic basis of political thinking in terms of its own environment, conditioning circumstances, and peoples. The long-established practice of blindly following the foreign gods is slowly, but effectively breaking down."[3] The Aprista emphasis, over a period of twenty-five years, upon the unique character of Latin America and its consequent need to devise ways of doing things in harmony with the tradition of her people may have helped to produce the more realistic trend seen by Professor Gil.

The Apristas understand that as long as millions of Indians continue to live on a subsistence level, and are not really incorporated into the life of the country, Peru will continue to stagnate. They insist, therefore, that Peru's great need is to teach the Indians to modernize their methods of farming, change their dietary habits, and participate in the life of the country. This may be a difficult task, but the Apristas draw inspiration from the achievements of the pre-Columbian civilizations and argue that the descendants of the builders of Chan-Chan, Cuzco, and Machu Picchu can recover the talents of their ancestors.

Whether the Aprista program can awaken the Indian and change his manner of living is unknown. The Apristas are convinced that it can transform the Indian into a modern man and liberate his genius, a genius which has been stifled by four hundred years of oppression. The speed with which other backward groups have adopted the techniques of modern society would support the Apristas in their belief. Dictatorship has always produced cultural paralysis. Its abolishment in Peru would at least enable the Indians to develop whatever capacities they have. If given the opportunity, they would undoubtedly display as much talent as any other group.

[2] "A Historian's Point of View," in William W. Pierson (ed.), "Pathology of Democracy in Latin America," *American Political Science Review,* XLIV (March, 1950), 101.

[3] In Pierson (ed.), *op. cit.*, p. 149.

From their study of history and their concern with the role of the Indian the Apristas have developed the theory of historical space-time. Although it is difficult for one who is not familiar with Professor Einstein's ideas on relativity to follow the Aprista reasoning, the theory appears logical and it throws much light upon historical development. As has been pointed out,[4] the theory of historical space-time is a product of the combination of ideas derived from modern physics and the Marxian dialectic. The Apristas insist that the Marxian program cannot be utilized under Peruvian and Latin American conditions. They are convinced, however, that the Marxian dialectic is a valuable tool, and they employ it by combining it with ideas derived from a study of Einstein's theory of relativity.

Few would dispute that the Apristas are correct in believing that the Marxian analysis no longer fits the contemporary world. Marx and Engels, in their writings, were describing the development of English capitalism as they saw it reflected in the material accumulated in the British Museum a century ago. Friedrich Engels' *The Condition of the British Working Class in 1844* and Karl Marx's *Capital* picture the kind of society against which the founders of the socialist movement rebelled. The Apristas correctly see that a program written for the English and Western European workers during the nineteenth century does not fit the needs of Latin America during the twentieth century. They certainly are not the only political thinkers to recognize that the Marxian doctrine does not apply to contemporary conditions,[5] but the Apristas seem to be unique in that they are the only group, until now, who have tried to use what they thought was valuable in the Marxist method of analysis. Building upon that, they have created a new philosophy of history.

The theory of historical space-time declares that each geographical area lives within a certain historic time which creates for each area its own historical space-time. Historical space-time is the total of all factors which combine to affect the life of a social group, combined in such a way that the total is greater than the sum of the parts. The point emphasized by the Apristas is that there is a certain "rhythm," or "spirit," or "collective consciousness" which each people develops as a result of all the influences to which they are exposed. This "X" quality which the Apristas call historical space-time motivates a people so they develop in a certain way despite the introduction of social institutions from

[4] *Supra*, pp. 30–34.

[5] Víctor Raúl Haya de la Torre sums up the Aprista viewpoint on Marx's ideas in "Latin American Letter," *Modern Review*, vol. 2 (June, 1948), 321–323.

another area. The Aprista contention that this explains why the Indian population of Latin America has not been integrated into the European culture of the ruling class appears to be valid. Peruvian society can be unified only when the institutions and laws take account of the character of its people.

Frederick Jackson Turner was able to revolutionize the study of United States history by pointing out that:

> ... the peculiarity of American institutions is the fact that they have been compelled to adapt themselves to the changes of an expanding people—to the changes involved in crossing a continent, in winning a wilderness, and in developing at each area of this progress out of the primitive economic and political conditions of the frontier into the complexity of city life.[6]

If the peculiarity of institutions in the United States was determined by the conquest of a continent and the conditions of life on an ever-moving frontier—which is generally accepted at this time—then Peruvian institutions are being molded by the conditions of life in that area. In this sense the Aprista ideas are an extension of Turner's theory and historical space-time is a name for the forces which affect the development of every social group.

The conclusion drawn by the Apristas from the historical space-time theory, that the angle from which one observes history helps to explain what one sees, is more easily demonstrable. Although Plato pointed out more than 2,000 years ago that men sometimes think they see things which are in actuality only shadows on a wall,[7] there are many who continue to take the shadow for the reality. The Apristas insist that the world looks different to an illiterate Indian living in an isolated valley in the Andes and to a Peruvian landowner living upon his income in Nice; each would desire a different program.

Recognizing the need for educating the oppressed Indians, the Apristas emphasize the fact that their movement must be more than a political party. The Apristas propose that their followers undergo a spiritual transformation, that they create the revolution within themselves. They stress this because they understand that as long as the majority of the Peruvian people remain illiterate, addicted to the abuses of coca and alcohol, diseased, filthy, and backward in every way, they can never remake the country no matter how many programs the Apristas write. As a result, the Apristas advocate honesty, an attempt by each person to develop a sound mind in a sound body, and the need

[6] *The Frontier in American History* (1920), p. 2.

[7] In the parable of the shadows on the cave wall. Book VII in the Benjamin Jowett translation of *The Republic*.

for each person to develop a social consciousness. The Apristas desire to make their movement an educational force, a way of life which appeals to the people. The people must make a personal transformation in order to be capable of transforming the economic and political organization of Peru.

This facet of the Aprista ideology is probably the most novel of all their ideas. Few other political movements have ever attempted activity of this kind. The Aprista ideas on this subject resemble certain of Gandhi's ideas, for Gandhi taught the close connection between ends and means and the need for the personal transformation. The Aprista leaders do the same and insist that a better Peru cannot be created without creating a people who are themselves better.

Their recognition of the close relationship between ends and means leads the Apristas to conclude that power must be achieved without violence. If Latin American politics is in need of anything it is less violence, and for recognizing this need the Apristas must be praised. It is true, of course, that various governments of Peru have accused the Apristas of being terrorists, of having assassinated many people, and of having attempted armed revolt. Language to justify violence in politics, however, cannot be found in the Aprista writings. Nor can incitation to revolt be found.

The two most cited examples of Aprista violence are the Trujillo revolt of 1932 and the Callao revolt of 1948. In 1932, the Apristas appear to have taken control of the city of Trujillo after a spontaneous revolt of the people expelled the central authorities. The central government bombed the city and used the army to recapture Trujillo, yet the Apristas took no action in the rest of the country. If they attempted a revolution in 1932, it was not organized by a national party. This also seems to be true of the events in Callao in 1948, when a naval revolt broke out and the central government overcame it. The Aprista party, which at the time held a majority in both the Senate and Chamber of Deputies, did not attack the government in any other part of Peru. If the Aprista leadership had anything to do with the events connected with the Callao revolt, they were the most inept revolutionaries on record.

On the other hand, the Aprista writings are consistent in advocating a peaceful achievement of power. When the Apristas wanted to protest the boycott of the Senate—which prevented the functioning of Congress in 1947—they organized a general strike in Lima and Callao. The strike was so successful that it was broken only by the imposition of martial law and the abrogation of the constitutional guarantees of civil liberty. The Aprista use of the general strike instead of a revolt at that time argues they did not believe in armed revolt as a political tactic.

The Aprista advocacy of democracy is a facet of its program which merits approval. The tyrants and the minorities, who benefit from undemocratic government, can never understand why a dirty, diseased, coca-drugged Indian should be permitted to vote or to organize in order to capture state power. The Aprista program is clear upon this issue. It advocates free elections, freedom of organization, and freedom of speech. The Apristas have faith that their ideas would win out if given the opportunity to be presented. In this period of world history when totalitarian ideologies have arisen and won millions of supporters, the Aprista insistence upon democracy will be endorsed by the friends of democracy whereas democracy's enemies will look upon Aprismo as an enemy.

The importance of Latin American resistance to imperialism is prominent in the Aprista ideology. Aprista ideas upon this subject are unique in that they combine opposition to imperialism with a recognition of Latin America's need for foreign capital. The Apristas object to having the national resources of Latin America owned and controlled by foreign interests. At the same time, the Aprista leaders suggest giving foreign interests a voice and a vote in the national economic congress they propose to create; they believe Peru should pay her defaulted foreign debt; and they desire foreign capital to come into Latin America. Aprista thinking on this subject appears to be contradictory at times, but it is based on realistic reasoning. The leaders of the movement understand that capital is an essential requirement for developing the Latin American economy, and they do not see any source for it other than the highly industrialized countries of the world. As a result, they advocate that foreign capital be welcomed in Latin America, but insist it should subordinate itself to the desires of the people.

Another distinctive feature of the Aprista ideas upon imperialism is their insistence that the United States and Latin America coöperate for their mutual benefit. The Apristas recognize that geography has made North and South America neighbors and, therefore, these two can either coöperate or have one dominate the other. The Apristas see only United States dominance in the past, but instead of advocating complete separation, they advocate coöperation as a policy for the future. They never fail to emphasize how much Latin America needs the United States and insist that each can benefit from a relationship based on mutual needs. This idea distinguishes Aprista nationalism from the type displayed by the Iranian and Egyptian nationalists in 1952.

The Aprista proposal that all the American states share ownership of the Panama Canal is also a reflection of their desire to see the United States and Latin America coöperate for mutual benefit. The Apristas think joint ownership of the canal would knit the twenty-one republics and serve as a symbol of inter-American unity. Joint ownership, they believe, would also strengthen the defenses of the canal.

It is not impossible that the future might bring conflict between the United States and Panama similar to the strife between Britain and Egypt over the Suez Canal. Any action which might prevent the possibility of such strife in the future would be valuable. The ideal situation would be United Nations' control of the world's strategic points—such as the Panama and Suez canals, Singapore, and Gibraltar. Because this is apparently impossible in a world split by a cold war, inter-American control of the Panama Canal is the only alternative to continued United States control. The Aprista proposal has much merit and would probably improve inter-American relations. Even token representation for the Latin American republics in the control of the canal would be of value.

Because imperialism is powerful, the Apristas believe that Latin America can successfully oppose its penetration only by itself becoming strong. They suggest that the way for Latin America to become powerful is for the twenty republics to unite. Unification of Latin America has been a vision seen by many since Bolívar first proposed it, but the Apristas are the first political thinkers to make it an important part of their program.

The Apristas are convinced that Latin America is a unit, the home of what they have called a "continental people." This contention apparently contradicts their claim that the area is populated by two different civilizations which should be integrated, but the Apristas see no contradiction. They argue that Latin Americans are a mixture of European and Indian ancestry combined with an unknown proportion of Negro. Although the exact racial composition varies among the republics, all contain people who are a mixture of these three basic elements. All twenty republics face the problem of integrating their populations, and the Apristas argue that this would be facilitated if the boundary lines were abolished.

The objection can be made that the people of Argentina do not consider themselves the same as the Haitians or the Paraguayans or the Bolivians. Despite this, the resemblance is present. The similarity among the people of Latin America could probably be more easily demonstrated by comparing similar classes in the various countries. A landowner in Peru resembles a landowner in Mexico or Argentina. A Peruvian Indian is not very different in his way of life from a Mexican or Bolivian Indian. A study of Latin America suggests that the differences among the people of the twenty republics are not great enough to justify classifying them as twenty different peoples. No one, for example, would argue that the Panamanians are different from the Colombians because the exigency of United States policy created a new republic in 1903. As the Apristas point out, Spanish is spoken by the majority of the population in all the republics except Haiti and Brazil. The Catholic Church commands the support of the overwhelming proportion of the population, and there is a certain rhythm which runs throughout all Latin America which gives the area a unified aspect.

Whether or not the Apristas are correct in looking upon all the people of Latin America as a "continental people," they are on sound ground when they advocate the political and economic unification of the area. It is becoming clear as time goes by that the stable and prosperous nation in the twentieth century will be large and populous. It is also clear that a large market is needed to provide the basis for any extensive industrialization. The example of the development of the United States is a telling argument for the advantages of unification. It contains within its borders many different kinds of people, yet the population of the forty-eight states regards itself as American. The attempt to establish a United States of Western Europe, the cooperation of the British Commonwealth of Nations, and the weakness of the small countries at the present time all point to the conclusion that the era of large and powerful states is emerging. It is to the Apristas' credit that they forecast this need as far back as 1924 and have continued to urge the unification of Latin America ever since.

The Aprista idea that Latin America needs the kind of over-all planning that is possible after unification is also one that is becoming more evident as the years pass. Planning has become the decisive factor in Western European defense and is becoming more decisive all over the world. Haya de la Torre pointed out to the author that if the economic development of Latin America were not planned, industrialization might lead to war among the various republics. He was particularly concerned about the efforts to begin the creation of a competitive steel industry in half a dozen of the republics. Steel, he said, means armament, and since no one republic—with the possible exception of Brazil—can provide a large enough internal market for a steel industry, the various countries may turn to conquest to win a market.[8] Another reason planning for Latin America is so important to the Apristas is that they recognize the magnitude of the problems in that area. The fact that these problems have not been solved until now seems to demonstrate that something more than a continuation of the status quo is needed for their solution.

The boundaries of most of the republics are a reflection of the colonial system. Each colony was in contact with Spain or Portugal and had little contact with its neighbors. Roads were constructed from each colonial center to the nearest seaport. In many cases, the roads which helped to knit the area before the Europeans arrived were destroyed or allowed to deteriorate. As a result, when independence came the population pattern of Latin America was spotty, with much uninhabited or sparsely populated area between each colony. Localism was strong, and the colonies became small republics instead of uniting as the thirteen English colonies to the north had done.

The Apristas may be too optimistic in hoping for one nation where twenty now exist. A more realistic solution might be the creation of several countries by combining the present republics. A United States of Central America would create a nation large enough to give most of the advantages of size without jeopardizing its creation by including too many of the present republics. The same would be true of other possible regional combinations. The Apristas are correct in advocating unification for Latin America because the trend of world events points toward the extinction of small states.

The proposals for the introduction of specific political, social, and economic reforms in Peru are another feature of the Aprista program that give it a revolutionary character. The introduction of even a small part of their suggestions would change the organization of life in the country. It is impossible to forecast how many of these specific proposals would be instituted if the Aprista movement ever were to achieve complete power. The leaders of the movement have read widely, traveled through many countries, and have studied the political and economic organization of many lands. Their reform program reflects this and contains ideas taken from many sources which they try to adapt to Peruvian conditions. The Apristas have good general ideas, but in their eagerness to have a suggestion for every aspect of Peru-

[8] Personal interview, April 1, 1948, Los Angeles, California.

vian life they become utopian at times. They propose, for example, that Peru immediately institute a modern merit system for recruiting government employees. This is a laudable objective, but the experience of other countries demonstrates that it is easier to propose a merit system than to create one. Their desire to give the Peruvians, through legislation, the kind of working conditions enjoyed only by workers in the most advanced countries is also visionary. This also can be said of their pledge to remove politics from the armed forces.

In spite of the utopian character of certain of the Aprista suggestions, most of their specific proposals would probably improve conditions in Peru. The most far-reaching effects would possibly come from an improvement of the educational system. Although it would be extremely difficult to accomplish, this would perhaps automatically produce many of the other reforms advocated by the Apristas. There have been dictatorial governments in countries where the people were educated (Germany is a prominent example), but there has never been a true democracy where the people were illiterate. This may be the reason the Apristas tried to carry their ideas about education into action by organizing night schools and by fostering legislation to improve education during the period from 1945 to 1948. Unfortunately, they never had the opportunity to institute all the changes they thought the Peruvian educational system needed.

Agrarian reform is a step advocated by many others besides the Apristas in Latin America. Its need is almost self-evident, because the latifundia system of landowning tends to prevent industrial progress in any country. When a small group owns most of the land it is usually inefficiently utilized and is generally devoted to market crops which bring a cash return. The production of crops for a world market is usually accompanied by a shortage of food within an agricultural country. This system also tends to keep farm workers uneducated and living in poverty. Agrarian reform is recognized by the Apristas as a prerequisite for democratic government. They understand that as long as a small group owns most of the land the status quo will find powerful supporters.

The desire for industrialization is not original with the Aprista ideology. Almost every political group in Latin America advocates industrialization, but the Apristas are different in that they insist industrialization must be planned. The Aprista ideas on this subject include a proposal for continental development in which free trade among the twenty republics can provide a mass market, whereas a tariff barrier around the area would protect industry in its developmental stage. The Apristas understand that industrialization is an essential prerequisite to raising the standards of living in Latin America. They propose that each of the twenty republics try to develop industries that can supply their neighbors and thereby aid industrialization through coöperation among the republics.

State ownership of certain industries, as advocated by the Apristas, is derived from their socialist ideas. They recognize that certain enterprises are so important that a modern country cannot permit them to remain under private ownership and control. In this the Aprista ideas are a reflection of the general tendency apparent in Western civilization where governments have progressively taken the ownership of more and more activities. This is true even in the United States, the world's most prominent example of private capitalism, where during the past one hundred years water, electricity, education, recreation, and other services have been in whole or in part taken over by agencies of the national or local government. In Europe this tendency has developed much further with railroads, telephones, coal mines, and many other enterprises owned and operated by various governments. There seem to be certain fields in which no government can permit private ownership to exist. Atomic energy, which is universally a governmental monopoly, is the classic example, for no government dares permit the private manufacture of atomic power. The Aprista movement recognizes this trend. It never advocates that the state take the ownership of all industry—as the Communists advocate, and as has happened in the Soviet Union—but it proposes state ownership in certain basic fields.

Aprista advocacy of coöperation as a method of conducting economic activity has two different roots. Most democratic socialist parties advocate the development of coöperatives, and the Apristas, who consider themselves democratic socialists, do the same. They also see that the Indian's insistence upon clinging to his communal method of landowning, the ayllu, makes it necessary to propose a method of proceeding that will fit the Indian. From this comes the Aprista idea that the ayllu should be developed into a modern, coöperative system of landowning. The Peruvian ayllu resembles the Mexican *ejido* which is a survival of the Aztec system of land tenure. Many Aprista leaders lived in Mexico for varying periods and had an opportunity to observe the attempts of the Mexican government to create the new ejidos, a form of coöperative farming. It is possible that this contact stimulated the Apristas to propose a similar arrangement in Peru.

The important weakness in the Aprista theory is its failure to answer the question of how to achieve power. The Aprista leaders try to make their movement an educational force, and they believe that eventually they can educate so large a proportion of the population that power will come to them. They always insist that they want to gain power through an election. Despite this emphasis, the Aprista theory does not seem to confront realistically the problem of the road to power. If the Aprista leaders think a dictatorship would eventually permit the Apristas to be voted into office, events until now have not justified this reasoning. The Apristas were permitted to nominate an Aprista for the presidency only once in the five elections held from 1930 to 1951, and that one time, in 1931, they were defeated by a fraudulent count.[9]

The keys to power in Peru are control of the executive branch of the government and the armed forces. Both are usually controlled by the President. Although the Apristas have demanded the opportunity to compete for the presidency in a fair election for twenty years, they have never been given the opportunity. The closest the Apristas ever came to power was in 1945, and then they were not permitted to run a member of the Aprista party for the presidency. It is, of course, possible that the Aprista leaders are good political theorists but poor political maneuverers. When they supported Bustamante and elected him to the presidency in 1945, they evidently thought that six years of legal activity would allow them to win the election in 1951 without difficulty. When Bustamante became President he refused to appoint Apristas ministers of the powerful executive departments. The Apristas, therefore, refused to participate in the first Bustamante cabinet, and the series of events began which led to the new dictatorship. A democratic election in which the Apristas could win the presidency was not held in 1951.

Even when elections are held in Peru, the majority of the population is disfranchised. Only about one in ten voted in the 1945 elections, which were the freest ever held in Peru. Since the Apristas appeal for support to the disfranchised majority, they should explain to them how power is to be achieved in a country where the majority is not permitted to vote. The Aprista writings never discuss the general strike as a road to power or the use of passive resistance, although Haya de la Torre applauded the use of the latter technique by the people of El Salvador. The Aprista movement will be forced to give attention to this question in the future if it is ever to achieve power.

[9] *Supra*, p. 13.

The Aprista ideas demonstrate that the movement is neither communist nor fascist although it has been accused of being both, sometimes by the same government officials. It is true that certain Aprista ideas have been used in a demagogic manner by Communists and Fascists, but the Aprista combination of ideas differentiates the movement from the two varieties of totalitarianism.

One of the best ways to label a movement is to identify its friends and its enemies. On this basis the Aprista movement falls among the progressive and democratic movements of our times. This is demonstrated by the fact that the Apristas are associated in the League of Democratic and Socialist Parties of America with such organizations as the Chilean and Argentinian Socialist parties and the Acción Democrática of Venezuela,[10] among others. None of these organizations are communist or fascist, and all have struggled for democracy and social progress in their countries. This is also demonstrated by the organizations with which the Apristas coöperate in the Inter-American Confederation of Labor[11] and the organizations represented at the Havana Inter-American Conference for Democracy and Liberty.[12] If being an enemy of communism makes an organization democratic, the Apristas qualify on this score, for the agents of the Russian government and the advocates of communism in Latin America have fought the Apristas since the organization was formed.[13]

Another clue to the Aprista thinking can be seen in what they admire and what they dislike. Aprista newspapers applaud the progressive forces and criticise and oppose the imperialists, Communists, and Fascists. *Trinchera Aprista* for 1937 and 1938, for example, supported the Puerto Rican nationalists; thought highly of President Lázaro Cárdenas of Mexico; supported the Loyalists in the Spanish civil war; applauded the election of President Pedro Aguirre Cerda in Chile; and supported the organization Young Cuba. At the same time, *Trinchera Aprista* criticized Rafael Leónidas Trujillo of the Dominican Republic, and opposed European fascism.[14]

---

[10] A good summary of the Acción Democrática ideas is found in Luis Lander, "La doctrina venezolana de acción democrática," *Cuadernos americanos,* LII (July–August, 1950), 20–39.

[11] *Supra,* pp. 89–90.

[12] On the Havana meeting see Andrés Eloy Blanco, "La conferencia de la Habana," *Cuadernos americanos,* LII (July–August, 1950), 73–75; Conferencia Interamericana pro Democracia y Libertad, *Resoluciones y otros documentos* (1950).

[13] See the bibliography of anti-Aprista writings by Communists, *supra,* p. 33, n. 49.

[14] *Trinchera Aprista, organo del Comité Aprista de México.*

The Aprista movement has never succeeded in winning the power that would enable it to put its ideas into practice. The strength of these ideas, however, is attested by the fact that more than twenty-five years of violent and continuous opposition from all defenders of the status quo, including the Army and the government, have failed to stifle either the ideas or the organization built to propagate them. Nor has the movement been a complete failure. Professor Samuel Guy Inman wrote in 1942: "Apra has already accomplished what should make all Peruvians proud of it. It has awakened young men in every American land to devote themselves to solving their countries' problems. It has brought a new appreciation of the importance of economic questions, of the place of the Indian, of the power of political organization, and the necessity of a clean life for those who would serve a noble cause."[15] Perhaps it is this which permits the Apristas to continue to repeat, "Solo el aprismo salvará al Perú," Only Aprismo will Save Peru.

[15] *Latin America, Its Place in World Life* (rev. ed., 1942), pp. 162–163.

APPENDIX A

[The Aprista Marseillaise, *Cancionero Aprista,* p. 6.]

I

Against the shamefaced past
a new doctrine rises in rebellion.
It is the true liberating ideal
which was founded in the crucible of truth,
which was founded in the crucible of truth.

We are covered with blood in history.
Our powerful and triumphal trail,
will give those who struggle tomorrow
a worthy example of action against evil.

Peruvians embrace
the new religion.
THE POPULAR ALLIANCE,
THE POPULAR ALLIANCE
will conquer
the coveted redemption.

II

As the APRA comrades live,
THE POPULAR ALLIANCE lives.
Militants pure and sincere,
we promise never to desert,
we promise never to desert.

Apristas to struggle
united to conquer!
Fervor. Action,
until our
revolution triumphs.
Apristas struggle
for our redemption!

APPENDIX B

[An example of Aprista slogans. The following appears on the inside front covers of various Aprista pamphlets, including Manuel Seoane, *Communistas criollos* (1933); Víctor Raúl Haya de la Torre, *Instructiva secreta a V. R. Haya de la Torre* (1933).]

Poster

It is necessary to seek the reality of America, not to invent it. We have a single powerful enemy, we should form a single powerful union.

Haya de la Torre.

Indoamerican Manual and Intellectual Workers

WE SHOULD STRUGGLE

AGAINST IMPERIALISM.

FOR THE UNION OF THE PEOPLES OF INDOAMERICA.

FOR THE NATIONALIZATION OF LAND AND INDUSTRY.

FOR THE REALIZATION OF SOCIAL JUSTICE.

AGAINST WAR.

AGAINST TYRANNIES.

ONLY APRISMO WILL SAVE US.

APPENDIX C

[Aprista code of action for youth. Partido Aprista Peruano, Federación Aprista Juvenil, *Código de acción FAJ* (1934), pp. 4–8.]

Apra youth: Prepare yourself for action and not for pleasure. This is thy law.

FAJISTA MORAL

1. AMA SUA—AMA LLULLA—AMA KELLA
2. With the austerity of your life, with your love of study, with your dedication to work, and with your generous example, conquer the obstacles which present themselves to you both within and outside the home. Persuade all those who attempt to stop you or to remove you from your organization that the FAJ is a school of morality, of energy, and of complete preparation for life.
3. Wherever you may be, be a missionary of the Aprista moral. Demonstrate to the comrades of the PAP that you are a true guardian of the great moral forces of the party. Struggle against doubt, against indecision, against inactivity, and against the lack of a feeling of responsibility.
4. Be sincere. Never fear telling the truth. A fajista never speaks in whispers.
5. When you give your word, keep it.
6. Be punctual in the completion of your duties and obligations.
7. Distinguish between strong language and foul language. Use the former, reject the latter.

FAJISTA SOLIDARITY

8. Nothing for me, all for a new Peru, just and free.
9. If you have entered the struggle it is because you are convinced that the supreme rule of your life should be to struggle for social justice and that only Aprismo can bring it.
10. Unity is the secret of the force of your great party. You, as a fajista, should never forget that you are an Aprista and that the members of the Party of the People are your older brothers. Look at them as such, but always keep guard that they are maintaining the spirit of our party.
11. The oppressed peoples of Peru, America, and the world are your brothers. Love them. For them thousands of Apristas died. Follow their example.
12. Offer your generous aid to the brother that needs it.
13. The interests of the United Front of manual and intellectual workers comes before your personal interests.
14. I save myself although the nation perishes is not a fajist maxim. Save the nation although I perish, is a fajist maxim.

FAJISTA PUGNACITY

15. Be brave, fair, and daring, but not cowardly or reckless.
16. Know that the Party is defended and that the Aprista state will be defended with action.

17. Believe in the struggle because that will produce everything. Support your organizations with your action. Be a constant sentinel; condemn energetically all incorrectness wherever you notice it.
18. Be an authentic soldier of the Aprista cause. Your iron discipline, your moral value, your decision to maintain alive the faith, and to strengthen enthusiasm for Aprismo should be seen at all times.
19. Be a disciplined and enthusiastic performer of the rules and slogans of your organizations.
20. Always remember that since the Aprista Party is an organization of struggle, the severest discipline and the strictest hierarchy of command should be observed and respected.
21. Be a guide and an initiator in acton. Do not lessen your participation in the spontaneous and devoted actions taught to you to be used against strange elements and saboteurs who betray the orders of your party.

Cultural Action

22. Without science there is no progress. Know that and, therefore, conquer yourself, prepare yourself, perfect yourself, teach yourself.
23. Teach him who knows less and learn from him who knows more. The knowledge you acquire is not for you alone; put it at the service of your organization.
24. Every day enrich yourself with more and more knowledge.
25. Study and know the doctrine of your party. Do not doubt any of it.
26. Know that if the community progresses, you must progress, and that if you progress, that will be an efficient element of progress for the community.
27. Make reading one of your primary habits. Do not devour books. Read them and apply their teachings. Always seek the origin of things, and do not be satisfied with the superficial.
28. Wherever you find yourselves defend the principles and the doctrine of Aprismo, which is progress and which, consequently, is a scientific movement.

Rules of Life

29. Be thoughtful more than regretful.
30. Be active, work with perseverance and tenacity. Be happy and optimistic.
31. Be realistic and not abstract; neither utopian nor wordy. Be clean and strong in your appearance.
32. Be unmerciful in criticizing yourself. Take the criticism of others and make use of it. Vanity is not found in the fajist mind.
33. Salute with the raised left hand the jefe of the Party as a tribute to the function which he exercises. In the same manner salute the members of the CEN when they address you and groups of comrades of the PAP or of the FAJ when they meet you or when they come near you.
34. When you should obey, do it without delays or reserves, for in this case obedience implies a division of labor which helps our cause. When you should command, every moment have the exact notion of your mission, of your responsibility, and of your duty as a leader.
35. Wherever you are, indoors or out of doors, conduct yourself in an exemplary fashion, so proving that Aprismo is, even in its outer manifestations, a complete renovation of personality.

36. Playing cards corrupts. Do not do it.
37. Select the shows you attend. Choose those that offer you healthful teachings and high artistic values and that give you lessons of morality and energy. Combat the frivolous and pornographic films.
38. The dance as art is worth cultivating; as a sport it is admissible; but reject the kind of dance that stimulates sensuality.
39. Do not squander your vitality. Put a rein on sensualism. Reserve your sexual energy. On your continence and health today depends the health of your children tomorrow. Condemn *Don Juanism.* If you feel attraction for a youth of the other sex, do not permit it to be translated into external manifestations of morbid and destructive sensualism. Dignify your sentiment, elevate it, utilize it as a lever pushing you to spiritual perfection, converting it into a source of collaboration and of stimulus of your Fajista work. The stimulation of the spirit does not destroy but creates. Do not forget that our country is sunk in corruption owing to the lack of true virility and authentic moral discipline.

Sanitary Rules

40. A healthy body is a guarantee of action.
41. Love the air, love the fields, love water, love nature.
42. Wash yourself. Guard your teeth. Clean your clothes.
43. Sleep enough. Do not stay up all night. Get up early in the morning.
44. Tobacco poisons. Do not smoke.
45. Coca, just as all poisons, kills your will. Do not chew it.
46. Alcohol degenerates the individual; it corrupts him. Do not drink.
47. Equalize your mental and physical improvement. Practice some sport, but remember that sport is a means and not an end. Do not be exclusively dedicated to it; also perform some intellectual gymnastics. Study.
48. Visit the FAJ doctor regularly and follow his instructions. Do not conceal your problems for he is your comrade and your older brother.

BIBLIOGRAPHY

THE FOLLOWING BIBLIOGRAPHY is a selected list of books, pamphlets, articles, and other material found useful in the preparation of this study. All items listed have been used.

The leaders of the Aprista movement have been prolific writers, but some of the published material has disappeared or is difficult to obtain because of the illegal status of the movement during much of its life. Despite this fact, enough material is available to obtain an understanding of the Aprista ideology and program.

GENERAL WORKS

BOOKS AND PAMPHLETS

BEALS, CARLETON. *America South.* Philadelphia, Lippincott, 1937.

Beals writes with an understanding of Latin America based on many years spent in the area, but at times is careless with his facts. Chapter 18 is a discussion of Aprismo.

———. *Lands of the Dawning Morrow.* Indianapolis, New York, Bobbs-Merrill, 1948.

An optimistic picture of the changes brought by the last war to Latin America. Pp. 289–296 are a sympathetic discussion of the Aprista movement.

BEMIS, SAMUEL FLAGG. *The Latin American Policy of the United States.* New York, Harcourt, Brace, 1943.

BLANKSTEN, GEORGE I. *Ecuador: Constitutions and Caudillos.* Berkeley and Los Angeles, University of California Press, 1951.

A scholarly study of political instability in Ecuador which helps one to understand Peru because of the similarities between the two republics.

BRYCE, JAMES. *Modern Democracies.* New York, Macmillan, 1921, 2 vols.

CARTER, ALBERT E. *The Battle of South America.* Indianapolis, New York, Bobbs-Merrill, 1941.

A survey of South America by a newspaper man who learned to speak Spanish and lived in the area for two years. The report of an interview with Haya de la Torre; pp. 280–286.

Almost every writer who visited Peru during the 1930's and early 1940's managed to interview Haya despite his living in hiding. The various impressions recorded as a result of these interviews help throw light upon the Aprista movement.

CONFERENCIA INTERAMERICANA PRO DEMOCRACIA Y LIBERTAD. *Resoluciones y otros documentos.* La Habana, the Conference, 1950.

The official report of a meeting in which the Apristas participated.

CRAWFORD, WILLIAM REX. *A Century of Latin American Thought.* Cambridge, Mass., Harvard University Press, 1944.

A valuable introduction to the subject. Includes a discussion of the ideas of González Prada and Mariátegui.

CUADROS CALDAS, JULIO. *El comunismo criollo.* Puebla, Pue., México, n. pub., 1930.

An attack upon communism by a Mexican writer who praises the Aprista movement. Chapter iv, "El Comunismo y el A.P.R.A."

DAVIS, HAROLD E. *Makers of Democracy in Latin America.* Washington, Inter-American Bibliographical and Library Association, 1945.

Biographical sketches of and short bibliographies about Latin American thinkers including Mariátegui, Haya de la Torre, and González Prada.

FERNÁNDEZ ARTUCIO, HUGO. *La organización secreta Nazi en Sudamérica.* México, D.F., Ed. Minerva, 1943. English edition: *The Nazi Underground in South America.* New York, Farrar and Rinehart, 1942.

An exposé of Nazi activity in South America by an Uruguayan political leader. The book is dedicated to Haya de la Torre.

FITZGIBBON, RUSSELL H., *et al.* (eds.). *The Constitutions of the Americas.* Chicago, University of Chicago Press, 1948.

Contains a translation of the Peruvian Constitution of 1933.

GARCÍA CALDERÓN, FRANCISCO. *Latin America: Its Rise and Progress.* New York, Charles Scribner's Sons, 1913.

GUNTHER, JOHN. *Inside Latin America.* New York, Harper, 1941.

A popular account which has been much criticized. The Aprista leaders state that the section dealing with their movement is accurate.

HERRING, HUBERT. *Good Neighbors.* New Haven, Yale University Press, 1941.

One of the best volumes interpreting Latin America to the average reader although the book concentrates on Argentina, Brazil, and Chile.

INMAN, SAMUEL GUY. *Latin America, Its Place in World Life.* Chicago, Willet, Clark, 1937; revised edition: New York, Harcourt, Brace, 1942.

Perhaps the best one-volume study of Latin America. The revised edition is practically a new book and contains a valuable bibliography.

INTER-AMERICAN EMERGENCY ADVISORY COMMITTEE FOR POLITICAL DEFENSE. Third Annual Report, First Section. *A Study of Conditions Necessary to Assure Political Defense.* Montevideo, the Committee, 1947.

The Committee points out the role democracy could play in strengthening Latin America. Many of the ideas resemble Aprista arguments on this subject.

JAMES, PRESTON E. *Latin America.* Revised edition. New York, The Odyssey Press, 1950.

A good geographical textbook.

JOSEPHS, RAY. *Latin America: Continent in Crisis.* New York, Random House, 1948.

A generally well-informed journalistic survey of conditions. Includes a report of an interview with Haya de la Torre.

LEAR, JOHN. *Forgotten Front.* New York, Dutton, 1943.

Includes a report of an interview with Haya de la Torre.

LINKE, LILO. *Andean Adventures.* London, Hutchinson, 1945.

MACKAY, JOHN A. *The Other Spanish Christ.* New York, Macmillan, 1933.

A study of the development of religious ideas in Latin America by a prominent Protestant. Mackay lived in Peru during the years the young students were developing their ideas. His intimate connection with Haya de la Torre and other Aprista leaders makes his observations valuable.

———. *That Other America.* New York, Friendship Press, 1935.

MAZO, GABRIÉL DEL. *La reforma universitaria.* Buenos Aires, Publicaciones del Circulo Médico Argentino y Centro de Estudiantes de Medecina, 1926–1927, 6 vols.

The most complete study made of the Latin American student movement of the 1920's.

MORLEY, CHRISTOPHER. *Hasta la vista.* Garden City, N.Y., Doubleday, Doran, 1935.

PRIVATERA, JOSEPH F. *The Latin American Front.* Milwaukee, Bruce, 1945.

Chapter xiv deals with Aprismo.

RIPPY, J. FRED. *Historical Evolution of Hispanic America.* New York, F. S. Crofts, 1932.

ROYAL INSTITUTE OF INTERNATIONAL AFFAIRS. *The Republics of South America.* London, Oxford University Press, 1937.

SPYKMAN, NICHOLAS JOHN. *America's Strategy in World Politics.* New York, Harcourt, Brace, 1942.

TOMLINSON, EDWARD. *Battle for the Hemisphere.* New York, Charles Scribner's Sons, 1947.

An eye-witness account of an Aprista mass meeting; p. 17.

ULLMAN, JAMES R. *The Other Side of the Mountain.* New York, Carrick and Evans, 1938.

UNITED STATES. DEPARTMENT OF STATE. *Ninth International Conference of American States, Bogotá, Colombia, March 30–May 2, 1948, Report of the Delegation of the United States of America with Related Documents.* Washington, Department of State Publications 3263, 1948.

WHITAKER, ARTHUR P. (ed.). *Inter-American Affairs, An Annual Survey.* 1941–1945. New York, Columbia University Press, 1942–1946, 5 vols.

WHITAKER, JOHN T. *Americas to the South.* New York, Macmillan, 1939.

A report of a conversation with Haya de la Torre; pp. 26–31.

WILGUS, A. CURTIS. *The Development of Hispanic America.* New York, Farrar and Rinehart, 1941.

ARTICLES

ALFARO, RICARDO J. "La intervención colectiva de la repúblicas americanas," *Revista de derecho internacional* (Habana), XLVIII (Dec., 1945), 153–162.

A reply by the Foreign Minister of the Republic of Panama to the proposal for collective intervention made by the Uruguayan Foreign Minister.

BLANCO, ANDRÉS ELOY. "La conferencia de la Habana," *Cuadernos americanos,* LII (July–August, 1950), 73–75.

A report of the Inter-American Conference for Democracy and Liberty held in Havana in 1950.

FRANK, STANLEY. "Some Cops Have Lovely Legs," *Saturday Evening Post,* vol. 222 (Dec. 24, 1949), 11–13, 39–40.

An article about the women in the New York Police Department containing the charge that the Aprista movement was connected with a narcotics smuggler convicted in a United States court.

HOLMES, OLIVE. "Army Challenge in Latin America," *Foreign Policy Reports,* vol. 25 (Dec. 1, 1949), 166–170.

A documented study of the army revolts in Peru and Venezuela during 1948.

JAMES, HERMAN G. "Government: Latin America," *Encyclopedia of the Social Sciences,* vol. 7, pp. 88–95. New York, Macmillan, 1932.

LANDER, LUIS. "La doctrina venezolana de acción democrática," *Cuadernos americanos,* LII (July–August, 1950), 20–39.

A description of the program of the Venezuelan political party which greatly resembles that of the Peruvian Apristas.

PIERSON, WILLIAM W. (ed.). "Pathology of Democracy in Latin America: A Symposium," *American Political Science Review,* XLIV (March, 1950), 100–149.

ROMUALDI, SERAFINO. "Labor and Democracy in Latin America," *Foreign Affairs,* vol. 25 (April, 1947), 477–489.

SALZ, BEATE. "Indianismo," *Social Research*, XI (Nov., 1944), 441–469.

SCHLESINGER, ARTHUR M., JR. "Good Fences Make Good Neighbors," *Fortune*, vol. 34 (August, 1946), 130–135, 161–171.

TANNENBAUM, FRANK. "Agrarismo, indianismo, y nacionalismo," *Hispanic American Historical Review*, XXIII (August, 1943), 394–423.

An excellent discussion of the status of the Indian in Latin America. Professor Tannenbaum writes with a thorough understanding of the area based upon years of study and travel.

WHITAKER, ARTHUR P. "Inter-American Intervention," *Current History*, vol. 10 (March, 1946), 206–211.

GENERAL MATERIAL ABOUT PERU AND PERUVIAN POLITICS

BOOKS AND PAMPHLETS

ACOSTA, JORGE. *Cómo ganar las elecciones de 1945*. n.p., n.pub., n.d.

Acosta was the general secretary of the Partido Comunista Peruano.

BASADRE, JORGE. *Perú: Problema y posibilidad*. Lima, F. y E. Rosay, 1931.

BAZÁN, ARMANDO. *José Carlos Mariátegui*. Santiago de Chile, Zig-zag, 1939.

A biography.

BEALS, CARLETON. *Fire on the Andes*. Philadelphia, Lippincott, 1934.

A sensational history of Peru.

BUSTAMANTE Y RIVERO, JOSÉ LUIS. *Tres años de lucha por la democracia en el Perú*. Buenos Aires, n.pub., 1949.

Bustamante attempts to justify his actions as president of Peru. He attributes Peru's regression to dictatorial government to the actions of the Aprista movement and exculpates his own.

CACERES, JOSÉ RAÚL. *El pasmo de una insurgencia*, (ensayo de interpretación de la realidad política peruana). Lima, Editorial Perú, 1941.

An anti-Aprista view of Peruvian politics; pp. 91–137 deal with Aprismo.

EGUIGUREN, LUIS ANTONIO. *El usurpador*. Lima, Talleres Ahora, 1939.

Mr. Eguiguren was elected President of Peru in 1936, but was not permitted to take office because the Apristas had voted for him.

GIURATO, TOTO. *Perú milenario*. Lima, Editorial Ecos, 1947, 3 vols.

A textbook history of Peru.

GONZÁLEZ PRADA, MANUEL. *Anarquía*. Santiago de Chile, Ediciones Ercilla, 1936.

González Prada's ideas greatly influenced the Apristas who consider him as a stimulator of their movement.

———. *Bajo el oprobio*. Paris, Tipografía de Louis Bellenand et Fils, 1933.

———. *Figuras y figurones*. Paris, Tipografía de Louis Bellenand et Fils, 1938.

———. *Horas de lucha*. 2d ed. Callao, Tipografia Lux, 1924.

———. *Nuevas páginas libres*. Santiago de Chile, Ediciones Ercilla, 1937.

———. *Páginas libres*. New edition edited by Luis Alberto Sánchez. Lima, Editorial P.T.C.M., 1946.

———. *Pensamientos*. Buenos Aires, Arco Iris, 1941.

———. *Propaganda y ataque*. Buenos Aires, Editorial Imán, 1939.

GONZÁLEZ VIGIL, FRANCISCO DE PAULA. *Defensa de la autoridad de los gobiernos contra las pretensiones de la Curia Romana*. 1848–1856, 12 vol.

INTERNATIONAL COMMITTEE FOR POLITICAL PRISONERS. *Political Prisoners Under the Dictatorship in Peru.* New York, the Committee, 1940.

The Committee was headed by Roger N. Baldwin and included Waldo Frank, John Haynes Holmes, Sinclair Lewis, Carleton Beals, and others.

MARIÁTEGUI, JOSÉ CARLOS. *7 ensayos de interpretación de la realidad peruana.* 2d ed. Lima, Editorial Librería Peruana, 1934.

One of the first books to stress the need for integrating the Indian into Peruvian society.

MEANS, PHILIP AINSWORTH. *Ancient Civilizations of the Andes.* New York, Charles Scribner's Sons, 1931.

A history of the origins of the Incas and a description of the organization of their society.

———. *The Fall of the Inca Empire.* New York, Charles Scribner's Sons, 1932.

NESTAREZ, FRANCISCO H. *Víctor Raúl Haya de la Torre y José Luis Bustamante y Rivero ante el proceso político histórico del Perú.* n.p., n.pub., 1945.

NILES, BLAIR. *Peruvian Pageant.* Indianapolis, Bobbs-Merrill, 1937.

PRESCOTT, WILLIAM H. *History of the Conquest of Mexico and History of the Conquest of Peru.* New York, The Modern Library, n.d.

RAVINES, EUDOCIO. *El momento político.* Lima, Ediciones Peruanas, 1945.

An anti-Aprista polemic by a Peruvian who belonged to the Aprista organization when it was first formed. In later years Ravines became an agent of the international Communist movement and a virulent opponent of Aprismo.

RODRIGA ALVA, VÍCTOR. *El mito de la revolución de agosto de 1930.* Lima, Imprenta Minerva, 1933.

SÁENZ, MOISÉS. *The Peruvian Indian.* Washington, Strategic Index of the Americas, 1944. (Translated and mimeographed by the staff of the Strategic Index of the Americas.)

Sáenz was Mexico's ambassador to Peru and had the opportunity to make extensive studies of the subject.

STUART, GRAHAM H. *The Governmental System of Peru.* Washington, Carnegie Institution of Washington, 1925.

UNSIGNED. *Conclusiones y resoluciones de la Primera Conferencia Obrera Regional del Sur.* Arequipa, Ediciones Sindicales Amauta, 1947.

This purports to be the opinion of a trade union, but reads as if members of the Communist party of Peru had written it.

———. *Dinamiteros del Chili.* Arequipa, n.pub., n.d.

This pamphlet is alleged to be the diary of an Aprista who spent his nights throwing bombs around Arequipa.

WIESSE, MARIA. *José Carlos Mariátegui.* Lima, Ediciones Hora del Hombre, 1945.

A biography.

ARTICLES

ARBAIZA, GENARO. "Benavides of Peru," *Current History,* vol. 48 (May, 1938), 15–17.

———. "South America's No. I Tyranny," *Current History,* vol. 49 (Oct., 1938), 26–29.

ARCA PARRÓ, ALBERTO. "Census of Peru, 1940," *Geographical Review,* XXXII (Jan., 1942), 1–20.

FRANK, WALDO. "A Great American," *Nation,* vol. 130 (June 18, 1930), 704.

An obituary of José Carlos Mariátegui.

———. "Two Peruvians: Dictator and Poet," *New Republic*, vol. 67 (August 12, 1931), 331–334.

Leguía is the dictator discussed; the poet is Mariátegui.

GALARZA, ERNESTO. "Debts, Dictatorship, and Revolution in Bolivia and Peru," *Foreign Policy Reports*, vol. 7 (May 13, 1931), 101–118.

INMAN, SAMUEL GUY. "José Carlos Mariátegui," *Collier's Encyclopedia*, vol. 13 (1950), 144.

A short biography.

MCBRIDE, GEORGE M. "Features of the Agrarian System of Peru," *Geographical Review*, XV (Jan., 1925), 137–139.

MIRKINE-GUETZEVITCH, BORIS. "Presidential System in Peru," *Political Quarterly*, vol. 5 (April, 1934), 269–272.

[MURPHY, CHARLES J.] "South America II: Peru," *Fortune*, vol. 17 (Jan., 1938), 48–60, 120–140. Translated by Alfredo Saco and José del Cueto as *El Perú bajo el oprobio, (La gran revista norteamericana "Fortune" enjuicia la tiranía de Benavides y al "Civilismo")*. Together with a report by Agencia Columbus on Murphy's interviews with Haya de la Torre and Benavides. México, Editorial Manuel Arévalo, 1938.

ROMERO, EMILIO. "La política del Perú en la república," *Cuadernos americanos*, XXXIV (July–August, 1947), 20–36.

STEWART, WATT. "A Peruvian Election," *Social Science*, vol. 13 (Oct., 1938), 319–325.

An eye-witness account of the 1936 election by a United States historian.

UNSIGNED. "Five-to-one-Favorite?," *Inter-American*, IV (July, 1945), 5–6.

———. "The Liberals Get a Candidate," *Inter-American*, IV (May, 1945), 11–12.

———. "The New Republic," *Inter-American*, IV (Sept., 1945), 9–10.

———. ". . . '95 Without Bullets," *Inter-American*, IV (August, 1945), 7–8.

———. "No Holds Barred," *Inter-American*, IV (June, 1945), 9–11.

———. "Peru's Coming Election," *Inter-American*, IV (Jan., 1945), 10–11.

MISCELLANEOUS

BELAÚNDE, RAFAEL. *Análisis del último mensaje presidencial*. Printed leaflet, dated March 19, 1948.

A criticism of President Bustamante by the President of the Cabinet and Minister of Government and Police from July 28, 1945 to January 23, 1946.

———. *Apostasía democrática del gobierno peruano*. Printed leaflet, dated Jan. 1, 1948. Reprinted from *Bohemia de la Habana*, Jan. 11, 1948.

An attack upon the Bustamante administration.

INTERNATIONAL COMMITTEE FOR POLITICAL PRISONERS. Copy of *Letter to Manuel Prado, President of Peru*, dated March 15, 1940 (Mimeographed).

The Committee asks President Prado to release the imprisoned Peruvian political prisoners.

UNITED STATES. COÖRDINATOR OF INTER-AMERICAN AFFAIRS.

Current Political Developments in Peru. Washington, Confidential Political Report number CR-105, Oct. 9, 1944 (Mimeographed).

———. *The Government of the Republic of Peru, A Constitutional Study*. Washington, Restricted Political Report number SR-131, Feb. 13, 1945 (Mimeographed).

———. *Present Political Situation in Peru, Summary*. Washington, Confidential Political Report number CR-103, August 28, 1944 (Mimeographed).

PERUVIAN GOVERNMENT DOCUMENTS

An English Translation of the Message of the President of the Republic, Dr. José Luis Bustamante y Rivero, addressed to the Peruvian Nation, on February 29, 1948. Lima, Emp. Tip. Salas e Hijos, n.d.

MINISTERIO DE GOBIERNO Y POLICÍA. *Los crímenes del Apra.* Lima, the Author, n.d.
An attempt to prove that the Apristas are murderers.

———. DIRECCIÓN DE PUBLICIDAD. *La verdad sobre el Apra, aprismo es comunismo.* Lima, the Author, n.d.
An attempt to prove that the Apristas are Communists.

———. *Terrorismo Apra.* Lima, the Author, n.d.
An attempt to prove that the Apristas are terrorists.

Notes Exchanged Between the Minister of Foreign Affairs of Peru and the Ambassador of Colombia Referring to the Asylum of Víctor Raúl Haya de la Torre. Lima, n.pub., n.d.

PERUVIAN COMMISSION OF INTER-AMERICAN DEVELOPMENT. *Reports Presented to the Conference of Commissions of Inter-American Development.* Washington, Inter-American Development Commission, 1944.
Contains valuable information about economic conditions in Peru.

THE WRITINGS OF THE APRISTAS

BOOKS AND PAMPHLETS

ALVARADO Z. ELIAS. *Episodios de la revolución Aprista de Trujillo.* Lima, Editorial El Sol, 1933.

EL BURÓ DE REDACTORES DE "CUADERNO APRISTA." *40 preguntas y 40 respuestas sobre el Partido Aprista Peruano.* Incahuasi, Editorial Indoamericana, 1941.
A propaganda pamphlet in which the Apristas try to explain their program in simple terms.

———. *La verdad del aprismo.* Incahuasi, Editorial Indoamericana, 1940.

CARNERO HOKE, GUILLERMO, and RICARDO TELLO N. (eds.). *Emancipación de la victoria.* Lima, Publicaciones de Prosa y Poesía, 1945.
A collection of poems and articles published to celebrate the Aprista electoral victory in 1945.

———. *Informes humanos.* Lima, Publicaciones de Prosa y Poesía, 1945.
Articles and poems by Aprista writers.

CHÁVEZ S., JOSÉ H. *Voces de la ruta heroica.* Lima, La Tribuna, 1947.
Poems and a play about Aprismo.

COSSIO DEL POMAR, FELIPE. *Datos biográficos de Haya de la Torre.* Lima, Editorial Américas Unidas, 1946.
An outline biography of Haya de la Torre together with forty-three interesting pictures.

———. *Haya de la Torre, el indoamericano.* México, Editorial América, 1939; rev. ed.: Lima, Ed. Nuevo Día, 1946.
A biography of Haya de la Torre by an Aprista who is a prominent artist and art historian.

COX, CARLOS MANUEL (ed.). *Cartas de Haya de la Torre al los prisioneros Apristas.* Lima, Editorial Nuevo Día, 1946.
Twelve letters from Haya de la Torre to Apristas who were in jail. The letters are

valuable as a source for Haya's ideas about clean living, personal morals, and the goals of the Aprista movement.

———. *Dinámica económica del aprismo.* Lima, Ediciones La Tribuna, 1948.

A collection of speeches and articles dealing with Peru's economic problems. Three draft laws advocated by the Apristas are reprinted in this book. One deals with the creation of a national economic congress; another would create a national financial corporation; and a third would create a Peruvian petroleum corporation.

———. *En torno al imperialismo.* Lima, Editorial Cooperativa Aprista Atahualpa, 1933.

DE LAS CASAS, LUIS F. *Unidad económica indoamericana.* 2d ed. Lima, Ediciones Páginas Libres, 1946.

An argument for the economic unification of Latin America by one of the younger Apristas.

FALERONI, ALBERTO DANIEL. *El aprismo y la lucha de clases.* Rosario, Editorial Continente, 1939.

An Argentine Aprista's discussion of politics. According to this book a Partido Aprista Argentina was in existence at the time.

———. *Frente único antiimperialista.* Rosario, Editorial Continente, 1938.

FEDERACIÓN APRISTA JUVENIL. *Declaración de principios, código de vida, marcha Aprista.* Habana, Editorial Apra, 1937.

A pamphlet published by the Aprista organization in Cuba.

FERGAC (ED.). *Aprismo.* Lima, n.pub., n.d.

A collection of speeches and articles by Haya de la Torre, Manuel Seoane, Luis Alberto Sánchez, Magda Portal, Pedro Muñiz, Carlos Manuel Cox, and Luis Heysen, all leaders of the Partido Aprista Peruano.

GARRIDO MALAVER, JULIO. *Canto a la navidad.* Lima, Ediciones Páginas Libres, 1945.

GONZÁLEZ CALZADA, MANUEL. *Juventud izquierdista de México.* Guanajuato, D.A.P.P. de México, 1938.

A Mexican Aprista describes the foundation of the Confederation of United Socialist Students of Mexico. Sections of the book are written by Fernando León de Vivero, Alfredo Saco, and Haya de la Torre.

HAYA DE LA TORRE, VÍCTOR RAÚL. *¿A dónde va Indoamérica?* Santiago de Chile, Ediciones Ercilla, 1935.

A collection of Haya's writings from 1927 to 1931.

———. *Ante la historia y ante la América y el mundo.* Buenos Aires, Editorial Libertad, 1932.

A copy of the verbatim report of the questioning of Haya de la Torre when he was in jail during the Sánchez Cerro regime. An excellent source for an authoritative expression of Aprista ideas because the questions dealt with Haya's opinions and beliefs.

———. *Construyendo el aprismo.* Buenos Aires, Editorial Claridad, 1933.

———. *El antimperialismo y el Apra.* 2d ed. Santiago de Chile, Ediciones Ercilla, 1936.

Haya's basic theoretical work in which he explains the general principles of Aprismo. Although it was written in 1928, lack of funds prevented its publication at the time.

———. *El plan del aprismo.* Guayaquil, Editorial Apra, 1932.

The *Plan de acción* adopted at the first national congress of the Partido Aprista Peruano in 1931.

———. *Espacio-tiempo histórico.* Lima, Ediciones La Tribuna, 1948.
Five essays and three dialogues in which Haya presents his theory of historical space-time.

———. *Ex-combatientes y desocupados.* Santiago de Chile, Ediciones Ercilla, 1936.
A collection of the periodical articles about Europe written by Haya from 1924 to 1931, the period during which he lived in Europe.

———. *Impresiones de la Inglaterra imperialista y de la Rusia Soviética.* Buenos Aires, Colección Claridad Acción y Crítica, 1932.
Contains a collection of Haya's periodical articles about Great Britain and Russia written from 1924 to 1927 and his "thoughts about the social and political reality of Latin America" dated from 1923 to 1929.

———. *Instructica secreta a V. R. Haya de la Torre.* Santiago de Chile, Editorial Indoamérica, 1933.
The same as Haya's *Ante la historia y ante la América y el mundo.*

———. *La defensa continental.* Buenos Aires, Ediciones Problemas de América, 1942.
A collection of articles written by Haya from 1938 to 1941 on the subjects of the war, continental defense, Pan Americanism, the unification of Latin America, and the inter-Americanization of the Panama Canal.

———. *La VIII Conferencia Panamericana ¿Otra comedia? Frente norte indoamericano contra la internacional negra fascista.* Santiago de Chile, Gutemberg, 1938.
An appeal to the Conference to do something about the Benavides dictatorship.

———. *Política Aprista.* Lima, Editorial Cooperativa Aprista Atahualpa, 1933.
Haya's writings and speeches dealing with Peruvian politics during the period from 1931 to 1933. Includes the *Plan de acción* adopted by the Partido Aprista Peruano in August, 1931, Haya's speech explaining the *Plan de acción* on August 23, 1931, his speech of December 8, 1931, and his manifestos to the Peruvian people of February, 1932 and November 12, 1933.

———. *Por la emancipación de la América Latina.* Buenos Aires, M. Gleizer, 1927.
Haya's first published book. Contains copies of his letters, speeches, and articles for the period from 1923 to 1927.

———. *Teoría y táctica del aprismo.* Lima, Editorial Cahuide, 1931.
A collection of Haya's writings from 1924 to 1930.

———. *Y después de la guerra ¿qué?* Lima, Editorial PTCM, 1946.
A collection of Haya's writings from 1942 to 1945.

HEYSEN, LUIS E. *Present y porvenir del agro argentino.* Lima, Ed. Librería Peruana, 1933.

———. *Verdades de a puño.* Lima, Empresa Editora La Tribuna S.A., 1947.

HIDALGO, ALBERTO, et al. *Radiografía de Haya de la Torre.* Lima, Ediciones Páginas Libres, 1946.
Six articles praising the accomplishments of Haya de la Torre published to celebrate his fifty-first birthday. The authors are Alberto Hidalgo, Antenor Orrego, Andrés Townsend Escura, Luis F. de las Casas, Manuel Seoane, Alfredo Hernández.

LEÓN DE VIVERO, FERNANDO. *Avance del imperialismo fascista en el Perú.* México, Editorial Manuel Arévalo, 1938.
A discussion of German, Italian, and Japanese influence in Peru.

MENESES, RÓMULO. *Aprismo femenino peruano.* Lima, Editorial Cooperativa Aprista Atahualpa, 1934.
On the role of women in the Aprista movement.

MUÑIZ, PEDRO. *Penetración imperialista.* Santiago de Chile, Ediciones Ercilla, 1935.

MUÑIZ, PEDRO, and CARLOS MANUEL COX. *Petróleo en Sud América, nacionalización o imperialismo.* Buenos Aires, Escuela de Estudios Argentinos, 1941.

ORREGO, ANTENOR. *El pueblo-continente.* Santiago de Chile, Ediciones Ercilla, 1939.
A discussion of the essential unity of the Latin American people. Orrego argues for continental nationalism and the correctness of the Aprista analysis.

PARTIDO APRISTA PERUANO. *El plan del aprismo, programa de gobierno del Partido Aprista Peruana y aprismo no es comunismo.* Lima, Editorial Libertad, 1933.

———. *El proceso Haya de la Torre.* Guayaquil, the Author, 1933.
The same as Haya's *Ante la historia y ante la América y el mundo.* A sixty-five-page preface is probably the best short account of the development of the Aprista movement by an Aprista.

———. FEDERACIÓN APRISTA JUVENIL. *Código de acción FAJ.* Lima, Editorial Cooperativa Aprista Atahualpa, 1934.
Rules of personal conduct for the guidance of Aprista youth.

SACO, ALFREDO. *Programa agrario del aprismo.* Lima, Ediciones Populares, 1946.
A detailed study of the Aprista agricultural and rural educational program.

———. *Síntesis Aprista.* Lima, n.pub., 1934.
One of the few attempts made by the Apristas to synthesize the Aprista philosophy and present it in an organized form.

——— and G. VEGAS LEÓN. *Partidos de frente único para Indoamérica!* México, Editorial Manuel Arévalo, 1938.
A polemic arguing that the Aprista program was more practical for Latin America than the popular front which was advocated by the Communists at that time.

SÁNCHEZ, LUIS ALBERTO. *Aprismo y religión.* Lima, Editorial Cooperativa Aprista Atahualpa, 1933.
A polemic against those who characterize the Aprista movement as antireligious.

———. *Carta a una indoamericana, cuestiones elementales del aprismo.* Quito, n.pub., 1932.
An explanation of how the Aprista movement was founded and why its program is needed by Latin America.

———. *Don Manuel.* 3d ed. Santiago de Chile, Ediciones Ercilla, 1937.
A biography of Manuel González Prada.

———. *Los fundamentos de la historia americana.* Buenos Aires, Editorial Americalee, 1943.
Sánchez's contribution to the philosophy of American history. He argues that the history of America is neither Indian or Spanish, but a mixture of both.

———. *Raúl Haya de la Torre o el político.* Santiago de Chile, Biblioteca América, 1934.
The best biography of Haya de la Torre.

———. *Un sudamericano en norteamérica.* Santiago de Chile, Ediciones Ercilla, 1942.
An account of Sánchez's trip to the United States.

SEOANE, MANUEL (ed.). *Autopsia del presupuesto civilista.* Buenos Aires, Comité Aprista Peruano, 1936.
A criticism of the Peruvian budget for 1935.

———. *Comunistas criollos (disección polémica de la charlatenería roja).* Santiago de Chile, Editorial Indoamérica, 1933.
Seoane's explanation of the difference between the Communist party and the Aprista party.

———. *El gran vecino.* Santiago de Chile, Editorial Orbe, 1942.
An account of Seoane's trip to the United States.
———. *La garra yanqui.* Buenos Aires, Editorial Claridad, 1930.
An attack upon United States imperialism.
———. *Nuestra América y la guerra.* Santiago de Chile, Ediciones Ercilla, 1940.
The Aprista argument for supporting the Western democracies during the Second World War.
———. *Nuestros fines.* 2d ed. Lima, Partido Aprista Peruano, 1931.
A speech explaining the Aprista program.
———. *Páginas polémicas.* Lima, Editorial La Tribuna, 1931.
A collection of editorials written for the Aprista newspaper *La tribuna* during the 1931 election campaign. Also includes a speech explaining the Aprista program made on August 10, 1931, to the first convention of the Partido Aprista Peruano.
———. *Rumbo argentino: Sondeos en el alma argentina.* Santiago de Chile, Ediciones Ercilla, 1935.
Seoane's observations on Argentina.
UNSIGNED. *Almanaque la tribuna 1948.* Lima, Emp. Ed. La Tribuna, n.d.
An almanac published by the Aprista newspaper *La tribuna.* Contains much information about the Aprista movement and program.
———. *Cancionero Aprista.* n.p., Editorial Apra, n.d.
A collection of twenty-two Aprista songs.
———. *Cartilla Aprista (léame y medite), por oneiros de AWIP.* Ecuador, n.pub., n.d.
A collection of short inspirational paragraphs about clean living and Aprismo.
———. *Los crímenes del Sancho-Civilismo, la revolución de Huaraz.* n.p., Editorial Claridad, 1933.
———. *Estatuto orgánico de la juventud Aprista peruana.* Lima, Comando Nacional de la J.A.P., 1945.
The rules governing the Aprista youth organization.
———. *Resoluciones de la convención de dirigentes del Partido Aprista Peruano, reunida en Lima, Perú, 1942.* Santiago de Chile, Comité Aprista Peruano de Santiago, 1942.
The resolutions adopted at an Aprista convention. A valuable source for official statements of the Aprista program.
VALCÁRCEL, GUSTAVO. *Apología de un hombre.* Lima, Ediciones Renovación, 1945.

ARTICLES

ALEGRÍA, CIRO, and ALFREDO SACO. "Japanese Spearhead in the Americas," *Free World,* vol. 2 (Feb.–March, 1942), 81–84.
An exposé of German, Italian, Japanese, and Spanish activities in Peru.
———. "30,000 japoneses forman la quinta columna del Perú," *Norte, revista continental,* vol. 2 (Feb., 1942), 14–16.
An exposé of Japanese activity in Peru.
COSSIO DEL POMAR, FELIPE. "Apuntes sobre el Indio peruano y su vida," *Cuadernos americanos,* XVIII (Nov.–Dec., 1944), 161–174.
An interesting discussion of conditions among the Peruvian Indians.
ENRÍQUEZ, LUIS. "A Latin Looks at Chapultepec," *Inter-American,* vol. 4 (April, 1945), 16–17.
A criticism of the 1945 meeting of the American states.

HAYA DE LA TORRE, VÍCTOR RAÚL. "An Inter-American Democratic Front," *Free World,* vol. 4 (Nov., 1942), 150–152.

———. "The Impressive Oratory of Mr. Wallace," *Free World,* vol. 6 (July, 1943), 20–22.

———. "Is the United States Feared in South America?," *Nation,* vol. 118 (April 9, 1924), 408–410.

———. "Latin America Fears Invasion," *Living Age,* vol. 359 (Oct., 1940), 146–149.

———. "Latin American Letter," *Modern Review,* vol. 2 (June, 1948), 321–323.
Haya sums up his thinking about Marx on the hundredth anniversary of the publication of the "Manifesto."

———. "Latin America's Student Revolution," *Living Age,* vol. 331 (Oct. 15, 1926), 103–106; same in *Bulletin of the Pan American Union,* vol. 60 (Nov., 1926), 1105–1108.

———. "Memo to U. S. Voters, an Editorial," *United Nations World,* vol. 2 (April, 1948), 64.

———. "The Mexican Revolution and its Problems," *Socialist Review* (London), new series, no. 13 (Feb., 1927), 24–29.

———. "Ciro Alegría's *El mundo es ancho y ajeno,*" *Ercilla* (Santiago de Chile), p. 22 (Dec. 3, 1941).
A book review.

———. "Toward a Real Inter-Americanism," *Free World,* vol. 3 (July, 1942), 163–164; same in *Mexican Life* (México), vol. 18 (Oct., 1942), 17, 50–51.

———. "What is the A.P.R.A.?," *Labour Monthly* (London), vol. 8 (Dec., 1926), 756–759.

HERNÁNDEZ ZELAYA, PEDRO. "Peru Moves Backward," *Nation,* vol. 168 (Jan. 1, 1949), 10–11.
Hernández Zelaya is a pseudonym for one of the Aprista leaders who writes of the Odría coup d'état.

SACO, ALFREDO. "El arsenal de la América Latina," *Norte revista continental* (New York, vol. 2 (March, 1942), 7.

SÁNCHEZ, LUIS ALBERTO. "A New Interpretation of the History of America," *Hispanic American Historical Review,* XXIII (August, 1943), 441–456.

———. "Anverso y reverso de los Estados Unidos," *Cuadernos americanos,* X (July–August, 1943), 19–28.

———. "Christianity and the Churches in Latin America," *Christendom,* vol. 9 (Winter, 1944), 40–49.

———. "El caso dramático de la América Hispánica," *Cuadernos americanos,* LIII (Sept.–Oct., 1950), 55–77.
One of the most recent expressions by an Aprista leader.

———. "Indoamérica versus Panamérica," *La nueva democracia* (New York), vol. 20 (June, 1939), 18–20.

———. "La enseñanza de la historia," *Cuadernos americanos,* LV (Jan.–Feb., 1951), 138–149.

———. "La participación de los alumnos en el gobierno universitario," *Cuadernos americanos,* XLVII (Sept.–Oct., 1949), 42–55.

———. "Latin America in the Post-War World," *Mexican Life* (México), vol. 20 (July, 1944), 15–16, 63–68.

———. "Latin America Warns the United States," *Free World,* vol. 1 (Nov., 1941), 135.

———. "Northern Exposure," *Inter-American Monthly,* I (May, 1942), 12–13.

———. "On the Problem of the Indian in South America," *Journal of Negro Education,* vol. 10 (July, 1941), 493–503.

———. "The Presence of Tradition," *Points of View, No. 4,* published by the Division of Intellectual Coöperation, Pan American Union, 1941.

———. "Sobre Gabriela Mistral," *Revista de América* (Bogotá), vol. 5 (Jan., 1946), 55–56.

———. "What's Left of Inter-Americanism," *Inter-American,* IV (Jan., 1945), 12–14, 39.

SÁNCHEZ, LUIS ALBERTO, and ALFREDO M. SACO. "Aprista Bibliography: Books and Pamphlets," *Hispanic American Historical Review,* XXIII (August, 1943), 555–585.

The best published bibliography on the subject.

SEOANE, MANUEL. "Conflict in Latin America," *Nation,* vol. 161 (Dec. 15, 1945), 654–655.

———. "If I Were Nelson Rockefeller," *Harpers,* vol. 186 (Feb., 1943), 312–318.

Seoane's suggestions about what the United States could do to improve inter-American relations.

———. "The Japanese Are Still in Peru," *Asia and the Americas,* vol. 43 (Dec., 1943), 674–676.

———. "Return of an Exile," *Inter-American,* I (Oct., 1942), 44–45.

———. "The South American Trojan Horse," *Nation,* vol. 155 (Nov. 14, 1942), 507–509.

———. "Where Do We Go from Here?," *Inter-American,* V (March, 1946), 23–25.

VÁSQUEZ DÍAZ, MANUEL. "El derecho de asilo y el caso Haya de la Torre," *Cuadernos americanos,* LV (Jan.–Feb., 1951), 75–87.

———. "El triunfo del aprismo en el Perú," *Cuadernos americanos,* XXIII (Sept.–Oct, 1945), 55–67.

APRISTA PERIODICALS

Apra (Lima). Organo del Frente Unico de Trabajadores Manuales e Intelectuales, Organo de la A.P.R.A. Vol. 1, no. 1, July, 1923.

Various issues in 1930 and 1934 used.

Apra (México). Boletín de la Sección Mexicana del Apra. Vol. 1, no. 1, Jan., 1935 to vol. 2, no. 2, March, 1936.

Apra (New York). Organo del Comité Aprista de los Estados Unidos. Vol. 1, no. 1, n.d. (1939?).

Faj. Edición clandestina contra la Tiranía, Feb. 22, 1935.

A mimeographed paper issued by the Aprista youth movement. N.p., but probably Lima.

Indoamérica. Organo de la Sección Mexicana del A.P.R.A. Vol. 1, no. 2, August, 1928.

La tribuna (Lima).

The chief Aprista newspaper. Issued as a daily whenever the Aprista movement was legal. Scattered issues used for the period from 1931 to 1948.

Sayari (Trujillo, Perú). Tribuna del Pensamiento Libre. Vol. 2, no. 8, Nov., 1946.

Trinchera Aprista (México). Organo del Comité Aprista de México. Vol. 1, no. 1, October, 1937 to vol. 2, no. 14, November, 1938.

MISCELLANEOUS

COMITÉ APRISTA PERUANO EN MÉXICO. *Carta abierta al director de "Excelsior."* N.p., the Committee, n.d. (Mimeographed).

COMITÉ DE DEFENSA DE LA CULTURA EN AMÉRICA. *Enemigo público No. 1 de la cultura en América.* N.p., the Committee, n.d.
A leaflet about the tyranny of Benavides, evidently of Aprista origin.

EL COMITÉ APRISTA DE MÉXICO. *¡Abajo caretas!* N.p., the Committee, 1937.
A printed leaflet.

———. *Pueblo de México.* N.p., the Committee, n.d.
A printed leaflet which charges that Benavides coöperates with Berlin, Rome, and Tokyo.

HAYA DE LA TORRE, VÍCTOR RAÚL. *Message to the Nation from Incahuasi, Perú, February 15, 1942.* Translated by the Office of Inter-American Relations, Stanford University, California (Mimeographed).

———. *México y el aprismo.* Incahuasi, Perú, August, 1938.
A copy of a four-page letter from Haya de la Torre to Licenciado Luis I. Rodríguez, Presidente del Partido de la Revolución Mexicana (Mimeographed).

LEÓN DE VIVERO, FERNANDO. *Letter,* written for the Comité Aprista de México addressed to the Señor Director de la Stanford University Libraries, dated April 26, 1938.

MATERIAL ABOUT THE PERUVIAN APRISTA MOVEMENT

BOOKS AND PAMPHLETS

ARISMENDI, RODNEY. *La filosofía del marxismo y el señor Haya de la Torre. Sobre una gran mistificación teórica.* Buenos Aires, Editorial Anteo, 1946.
An Uruguayan Communist argues that the theory of historical space-time is proved wrong by Marxism-Leninism-Stalinism.

GUARDIA MAYORGA, CÉSAR A. *Reconstruyendo el aprismo. Exposición y crítica de la doctrina política y filosófica hayista.* Arequipa, Perú, Tip. Acosta, 1945.
A Communist polemic against the Aprista ideology.

MARTÍNEZ DE LA TORRE, RICARDO. *Apuntes para una interpretación marxista de historia social del Perú.* Lima, Empresa Editoria Peruana S.A., 1947.
A Communist attack upon the Aprista movement.

MELLA, JULIO ANTONIO. *La lucha revolucionaria contra el imperialismo, ¿qué es el ARPA?* [*sic*]. México, n.pub., 1928.
The first Communist attack upon the Aprista movement. Written by a Cuban Communist, it has been widely distributed in several editions by the Communist apparatus.

UNSIGNED. *El verdadero plan de la Alianza Popular Revolucionaria Americana.* N.p., Editorial Pachacutek, n.d.
An anti-Aprista propaganda pamphlet which attempts, by quoting Haya de la Torre, to prove that the purpose of the Aprista movement is to establish "communism" in Peru.

———. *Los documentos comprobatorios de la dirección comunista del Apra, la prueba de que la Alianza Popular Revolucionaria Americana es una secta extranjerizante, que conspira contra la nacionalidad peruana.* Lima, Imprenta Popular, 1932.
Three letters written by Haya de la Torre in 1929 and 1930 published with interpolations to prove that Aprismo and communism are identical.

———. *Proceso aclaratorio de la traición de Esmaro Salas al Partido Aprista Peruano.* Lima, Empresa Tipográfica Nacional, n.d.
Esmaro Salas was expelled from the Partido Aprista Peruano. In this pamphlet he argues that he was unjustly expelled and that the party is undemocratically controlled.

VARGAS, JUAN. *Aprismo y marxismo.* Buenos Aires, Editorial Claridad, 1936.
A Communist polemic arguing that the Aprista movement is a "petty bourgeois and reactionary organization."

ARTICLES

ALEXANDER, ROBERT J. "Aprismo—is it Socialist?," *Modern Review*, vol. 1 (Nov., 1947), 682–690.

———. "Haya de la Torre Hides Again," *Canadian Forum*, vol. 29 (May, 1949), 31–33.

———. "The Latin American Aprista Parties," *Political Quarterly*, XX (July, 1949), 236–247.
Contains a list of the various organizations in Latin America which have programs similar to that of the Peruvian Aprista movement.

BEALS, CARLETON. "Aprismo; the Rise of Haya de la Torre," *Foreign Affairs*, vol. 13 (Jan., 1935), 236–246.

DE BERNASCHINA, MARIO. "Entrevista con Haya de la Torre," *Revista de América*, Boston, Ginn, 1943.

FLETCHER, WILLIAM GLOVER. "Aprismo Today; an Explanation and a Critique," *Inter-American Quarterly*, vol. 3 (Oct., 1941), 14–20.
Haya de la Torre criticized this article for giving a false impression of the Aprista movement.

JAMES, EARL K. "Apra's Appeal to Latin America," *Current History*, vol. 41 (Oct., 1934), 39–44.

JOSEPHS, RAY. "Uncle Sam's Latin Salesman," *Collier's*, vol. 122 (Oct. 16, 1948), 62–67.
Josephs calls Haya de la Torre "Uncle Sam's Latin Salesman." There are many inaccuracies in Josephs' article.

MACKAY, JOHN A. "A Voice from a Peruvian Prison," *Missionary Review of the World*, vol. 56 (Dec., 1933), 584–585.

MANCHESTER, HARLAND. "Haya of Peru," *Survey Graphic*, vol. 37 (Jan., 1948), 8–11, 37–38.

MANDULEY, LYN SMITH. "The People's Warrior," *Inter-American*, V (Nov., 1946), 18–20, 30–32.

MCNICOLL, ROBERT EDWARDS. "Intellectual Origins of Aprismo," *Hispanic American Historical Review*, XXIII (August, 1943), 424–440; reprinted as "Origines intelectuales del aprismo," *Político* (Habana), vol. 2 (May, 1944), 14–25.

MURKLAND, HARRY B. "Peru's Peaceful Revolution," *Current History*, vol. 9 (August, 1945), 94–98.

PEDROSA, MARIO. "The Voice of South America," *Common Sense*, X (March, 1941), 67–70.

PULGAR VIDAL, JAVIER. "Democracia y comunismo," *Cuadernos americanos*, L (March–April, 1950), 18–30.

———. "La teoría del 'Reto Respuesta' de Toynbee y el espacio-tiempo-histórico," *Cuadernos americanos*, LIII (Sept.–Oct., 1950), 108–134.

SELVA, SALOMÓN DE LA. "La unión de las Americas," *Cuadernos americanos*, VI (Nov.–Dec., 1942), 50–52.

UNSIGNED. "Haya de la Torre expone el peligro del comunismo," *La Opinión* (Los Angeles), April 4, 1948, pp. 1, 7.

A report of Haya's speech at a meeting in Los Angeles, California, supporting the government of Costa Rica against the rebellion of 1948.

———. "The Story of Haya de la Torre," *Nation*, vol. 118 (April 9, 1924), 406–407.

PRINCIPAL PERIODICALS

Amauta (Lima). Vol. 1, no. 1, September, 1926. Ceased publication after vol. 4, no. 32, Sept., 1930.

José Carlos Mariátegui was the editor until he died. Haya de la Torre and other Apristas contributed to *Amauta*.

Andean Air Mail and Peruvian Times (Lima).

A news weekly in English. Used for 1945 to 1950 inclusive.

Cuadernos americanos (México). Bi-monthly. Established Jan., 1942.

Used for 1942–1951.

The Inter-American (Washington). Monthly. Vol. 1, no. 1, May, 1942. Ceased publication with vol. 5, no. 11, Nov., 1946.

The New York *Times* (New York). Daily.

Used for 1920–1948.

INDEX